A Bird in the Hand

Bill Doherty

CONTENTS

ILLUSTRATIONS

To my late father

Without him, I would have been nothing;
without his help, I would have achieved little;
and without his guidance, I would have got nowhere.

Always by my side

INTRODUCTION

The practice of bird-trapping was outlawed in Great Britain many years ago. Since then, it has steadily faded into a part of avian history that most legitimate bird-keepers would want to forget. There still exists a tiny underground movement of bird-trappers in this country, where individuals pursue their illicit activities chiefly for financial gain. In banning taking birds from the wild, legislation deprived people who boasted a genuine affinity for our feathered friends of their hobby, while leaving us with a scab of semi-professional catchers whose only interest is money.

One day, it occurred to me that nobody had dared to write about bird-trapping before in any form or guise – not the horrible, cruel times depicted in various Thomas Hardy writings or the cash-driven, bird-dealer era of today, but that short period when our forebears were beginning to realise that they were bird-lovers and how interesting the closer study of birds in the wild and in captivity could be.

The fear of reprisals from various avian organisations or wildlife and conservation bodies, or the damning of their work as a handbook for bird-trappers will have put off many authors who might otherwise have enlightened or entertained us. I decided to take up the challenge of furnishing the bird world with such a manuscript, to provide an account of what went on, and to some extent why, even though the time I write about was the transitional period shortly after the first of the principle wildlife and countryside laws was implemented.

I have endeavoured to chronicle through the eager eyes of youth a collection of my memories, which are in their own way a quite unusual record of activities. I have gone over the past for just the right people to accompany me on my journey and have included a varied cast of characters. To these I have added a faithful canine companion, true incidences – some happy, some sad – interesting observations on wildlife and a drip-feed of educational tips for the would-be bird-lover. I have also included some local interest in the form of descriptions of the beautiful area of Northumberland where I was brought up and accounts of bygone days that will hopefully jog many memories.

I write as a bird-lover, an aviculturalist, a country diarist and established author of many articles in national avian publications. I have studied this country's wonderful wildlife all my life, and there has never been a dull moment during my wanderings on which I may see what others may often miss. My bird-keeping life has also given me a great deal of pleasure, and I have been able to draw from it for the purposes of research.

The word cruelty is often bandied about as a politically-correct vote catcher whenever the subject of bird-trapping is raised, but in over 30 years, which includes the period of my adolescent finch-catching activities, I can say categorically that I have never witnessed a single act of cruelty – although my definition of the word may differ from others'. These days, I do not practice what I was taught in the field, not because I think it would be cruel, but because it is against the law of the land. Being subjected to large fines or even custodial sentences is not what I want to get from my life with birds.

Long before the introduction of the 1954 Protection of

Birds Act went most of the way towards banning taking birds from the wild, the trapping of finches used to be practised countrywide. Common finches such as linnets, goldfinches and chaffinches were caught and prized for their beautiful singing and also for their ability to adapt quickly to life in captivity.

Almost every home possessed a singing bird of some description but, further back in our history, all wasn't peaches and cream. To craft birds into becoming even better songsters, some brutal practices took place, such as 'blinding', where chaffinches would have their eyelids carefully sealed by cauterisation with the edge of a red-hot pin. The birds were kept for the rest of their lives in confined spaces; they sensed where their food and water sources lay and, through practice, didn't starve. This pitiless tradition did enhance the birds' singing prowess, but at a terrible cost. To this bird-lover, this was truly cruel.

Even further back, small passerines used to be caught for food and, in some European countries, this continues unabated. We can only imagine the vast numbers of finches and other species that were indigenous to our green, but perhaps not so pleasant lands, at that time – before intensive farming practices took hold, before the removal of ancient woodland and hedgerows, and before the blight of toxic weed-killers and pesticides poisoned our birds and the insect life they depend on.

People were generally poor then, and the times brutal and hard. Common folk made full use of what was on offer, and it is recorded that roasts of skylarks, starlings and finches were eaten, while pickled blackcaps, whitethroats and warblers were seen as delicacies.

Thankfully, genuine cruelty, together with the mass

slaughter and consumption of birds that possess little or no nutritional value, gradually disappeared, but the trapping of birds as pets or for avicultural purposes went on, and still does, although in both cases wild birds are now of little real value. Through controlled management and the ability of dedicated breeders, finches produced in captivity are far superior in many ways to their wild counterparts. Catching wild birds and then adding them to a breeding program of exhibition stock might have a disastrous effect and would be of limited worth genetically.

If a singer or pet for the house is sought, these genetically-modified examples would again meet all requirements. Furthermore, there are many canary varieties or hybrids in existence today that are far more suitable as pets.

Nowadays, the few remaining trappers make their profits by catching wildlings and stretching aluminium rings onto their legs. The rings are then crimped to their original size with specially adapted pliers, and the birds sold on to unsuspecting buyers, who believe they have bought genuine aviary-bred birds. Such specimens can change hands for hundreds of pounds in some cases.

Time is nearly up for the bird-catcher. Society now has an arsenal of technology at its disposal to track and detect trappers or birds that are held illegally, although this can sometimes involve modern-day, witch-finder generals from an army of so-called experts travelling the country and raiding the birdsheds of dangerous pensioners, who have been suspected of being trappers or the perpetrators of other hideous wildlife crimes.

The old school of birdmen may have all but disappeared into the mists of time but, whether we like it or not, their ghosts remain as part of our history. This book is an irreverent but accurate account of the ways of some of these people, men who became an integral part of my childhood and who indirectly influenced my later life. It is not, and never was, intended to be a handbook for bird-trappers, but a fitting testimony to some old friends who loved their birds and who, like me, could never envisage their lives without wildlings to observe or a bird in the hand.

CHAPTER I

THE BLUE TOUCH-PAPER IS LIT

Awakened from deep slumber and with focus only partially restored, I began to study the wallpaper that
surrounded my bed like a flower-patterned scarf. If stared
at for a period of time, the detailed red roses would trans-
form magically and resemble the heads of soldiers wearing
tin hats or turban-clad, far-eastern fakirs staring back at me
with piercing eyes.

As shafts of January sunlight began to stream through
the narrow gap in the curtains, I lay sprawled across the bed,
my enquiring mind investigating the sources of the various
types of conversations and sermons that drifted through
the metal-framed window: the yaffle of starlings squabbling
over a plateful of bread crumbs my mother had thrown onto
the bare garden; a song-thrush addressing the surroundings
from his pulpit with his cheerful soliloquy, a chorus that
seemed to ask, Did he do it, did he do it?

My finely-tuned hearing was suddenly diverted from the
velvet world I was bathing in and redirected towards sounds
emanating from below: deep, blurred voices, like bitterns
calling from dense reed-beds, drifted upwards through the
floorboards.

Like a quick-footed hare, I darted from under the warm
blankets, the pink candlewick bedspread and Dad's trench-
coat – the heavy, full-length, army coat, faded, torn and
medalled with brass buttons, was a luxury shared between

and sometimes fought over by my sister and me during the long, cold winter nights. I stumbled as I frantically pulled on my grey, short trousers. I grabbed a shirt from the back of the chair and had it on, buttoned up and tucked in before I was halfway down the steep stairs. At the bottom, I paused, my trembling hand on the bulbous, brass knob that would twist out of shape the reflection of any face that had the audacity to look at it. I was straining to hear what the distorted voices were saying, and my curiosity soon replaced any apprehension I felt. I summoned up the courage to open the panelled door and stole into the living-room, like Oliver Twist on his quest for more.

My father stood sentinel in front of the tall, black cast-iron fireplace, warming his backside with the heat from the dancing flames. He turned and, with a proud, fatherly grin, introduced me to the two swarthy-faced visitors sitting there.

'This is wor Bill.'

Both men were dressed in dark attire. One was tall, thin and young; his black, well-greased hair was swept to one side. He had quite a large nose, and I had the desire to duck down when his big front teeth thrust themselves in my direction as he greeted me with a smile.

The second man was much older, and his fragile-looking frame suggested he could easily have been the runt of the litter. Even when sitting, his delicate frame was well bent and stooped. The skin of his friendly face was brown and deeply wrinkled; it was well-worn, time-wounded and scarred, but full of character. His hair was dark like his friend's, but thicker, windswept and untidy.

The younger man wore mud-covered, black Wellington boots, a fact that didn't go down too well with my mother.

On entering the room, she stared down disapprovingly at the brown dirt left on her proggy mat, which lay in front of the hearth like a hunter's trophy, and then she stomped out muttering terms of disapproval under her breath.

The older chap leaned forward.

'Hello there, youngin! Yer dad tells me you're an up-and-coming birdman. What's yer favourite birds?' My wide eyes glanced sharply towards Dad, and then quickly back to a face waiting patiently for an answer.

'Goldfinches,' I replied, tersely.

'Good choice,' he said, and the old fellow went on to explain that, as well as goldfinches, he kept bullfinches, linnets and peachies – the Northumbrian nickname for lesser redpolls. I couldn't believe it. His face broke into a grin as he witnessed my obvious excitement, and he delivered some additional bird snippets to feed my enthusiasm.

Before I could pose a myriad of questions, my dad began to build a wall of conversation that was to block me out, temporarily. This was my cue to keep quiet for the time being. I would have to plan this well, or risk getting relegated to the kitchen with my mother. I paid little attention to the trio's discussion: I was trying to think how I could safely get their attention.

Like the electric, blue dart of a kingfisher, a flash of inspiration entered my head. With the true bushcraft and stealth of a country boy, I made my way slowly but surely to the sideboard at the back of the room and gently slid open the top drawer. This was my favourite drawer, and I always relished rummaging around this Aladdin's Cave of useful trinkets, knick-knacks and curios. Every time I explored its contents I seemed to find some new and interesting treasure – unlike the bottom drawer that was full of all kinds of junk:

odd socks with gaping holes, half-used balls of knitting-wool that bound together everything else in the drawer, dye-cast Matchbox cars whose wheels had been removed out of curiosity. Quickly, I pulled aside the accumulated collection of items. That's what I was looking for – my Ladybird book of birds.

Like a mountaineer on a narrow ledge, I inched over and took up a strategic position on the edge of the settee, where the older man could see that I was holding some mysterious, secret possession. I opened my book at a page showing a beautiful, pastel drawing of a pair of bullfinches sitting on branches decorated with snow. I placed the hardback on my lap, continuously closing and reopening it, like a bower-bird display, to seize the older man's attention.

Eventually, my well-laid plan paid dividends. With an inquisitive expression, the old man looked across.

'What you got there, lad?' Without a word, I opened the book fully and passed it to the spindly, outstretched hand. I watched his shaggy eyebrows lift while he viewed the pages, then stop with the book open, his index finger acting as a bookmark. He showed me the picture.

'Ave got a bullfinch cock like that one,' and he passed the book to the younger man. His friend gazed at the open pages, his eyes widening, acknowledging the beauty of the bird he was looking at.

'It's better than that,' he countered. My bottom jaw dropped.

'Where did you get him?' I asked. The old man butted in,

'Caught him.' My excitement was now uncontrollable, as I screeched,

'Dad, he said he caught it!' My father scowled lightly in my direction.

'Calm doon, Willie!' When he referred to me as Willie, in

a voice edged with measured grandiloquence, coupled with an uncompromising look of displeasure, I knew I'd better do as I was told.

The stranger browsed through the pages again.

'Caught them.' He turned another page. 'Caught them.' He returned my book with a number of pages grouped together. Quickly, I looked and found pictures of linnets and goldfinches. Excitedly, I leapt up and ran into the scullery to show my mother.

'Mam, Mam! Look at these! Those blokes in there catch birds. Look, look at these! These are what they catch.' My mother turned, stiff-necked, and stooped towards me.

'Lovely,' she said laconically. Mam obviously didn't share my enthusiasm for birds at that time and began playing a game of chase-me with the mixed vegetables that bobbed in the deep-sided, stone sink.

I turned sharply on hearing Dad and the two men enter the scullery behind me. They were partly in conversation and laughing as they approached. As the old man brushed past, he whispered in a secretive voice, out of the corner of his mouth,

'Get yer dad to fetch you up to my place to see my birds one day,' and he rubbed the top of my head vigorously with his claw-like hand. In tandem, both men bid farewell politely to my mother. She, in turn, glanced slowly over her shoulder.

'Bye,' she replied quietly. I got the distinct impression she didn't care much for our scruffy, early morning guests.

When Dad returned from seeing them away, I immediately asked who they were.

'The old one was Jimmy Miller the Ragman, the other his son, Dicky.'

Now, ragmen were a unique breed that always interested and intrigued me so much. Some were of Romany descent; others had a more amoral and unscrupulous tinker background. They travelled with horse and cart around the streets of Bedlington, where I lived in my youth, collecting old clothes or scrap-iron. Their unique and unpronounceable call would echo around the housing estate, proclaiming their arrival. In exchange for a reasonable bundle of unwanted garments, a payment of wooden washing-line pegs or a handful of colourful balloons would be made. The kids of today will never experience the excitement of chasing after the ragman's cart, through streets, narrow lanes and over cobbled roads, or the joy in feeling those balloons being pressed firmly into the palms of their hands.

This was my first encounter with old Jimmy Miller, but I was to have a lengthy, fruitful relationship with him through bird-keeping and loitering around green fields and dense woods where wild birds hang out. Dicky, well, I later accompanied him into various forms of poaching, but for now it's the old man's tale I have to tell.

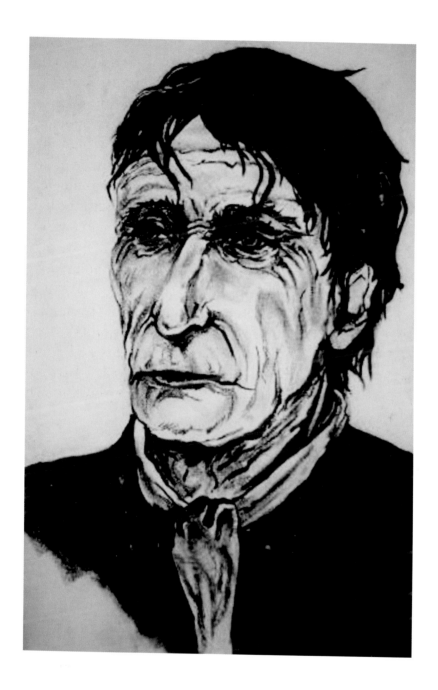

CHAPTER 2

JIMMY THE RAGMAN

Seven long days had passed since the Millers' visit. I swear a custodial sentence of hard labour would have passed more swiftly. During that week, I must have been the bane of my father's life, plaguing him incessantly to fulfil Jimmy the Ragman's invitation for me to see his birds. I was beginning to doubt whether the offer was genuine. Surely, Dad wouldn't put me off like this, unless they had been having me on. But it was approaching my 11th birthday; maybe this would help secure a visit.

Another week passed. It was a bitterly cold, Saturday morning, the eve of my birthday on the 26th of January. While I was in the garden feeding our collection of rabbits and chickens, I heard Dad calling for me from the house. I had two particular favourite bantams at that time, Ginny and Bridget Mary – names bestowed upon them by my father. I always made a general fuss over these two birds, sometimes having to fight off the attentions of their gallant cockerel. My friendship was rewarded with an endless supply of eggs. At the same time every day, I collected their small but tasty produce, always between 4.45pm and five o'clock in the afternoon.

I cleared my throat and spat in the direction of the strutting, scratching pair – it landed on the hard, bare garden, that was still partly decorated by Jack Frost's wanderings. Both birds quickly ran forward and pecked at my sputum

– I laughed and threw them an extra handful of corn, as I bade my temporary farewell.

In the scullery, Dad was standing next to my mother. He held a glass of milk in one hand and, in the other, a half-eaten slice of bread that he had recently dipped in the belly-rumbling juices of the meat slowly cooking in the oven.

'Are we going to Jimmy Miller's?' This was the first question that had entered my head. With a loud gulp, Dad finished his milk and put the empty glass on the draining-board.

'You will see. Just get your coat.' And he left the house by the back door.

'Bye, Mam. I think we're going to see Jimmy Miller's birds.' Running out of the door, I heard my mother's voice raised in concern.

'Don't forget your Balaclava! It's cold outside.' This spurred me on to run even faster to catch up with Dad, who was already at the bottom of our yard.

I hated wearing a Balaclava; it irritated me so much. I was forever pulling and stretching the chin-piece out of shape, in a futile attempt to obtain some respite from the coarse, woolly material rubbing against my tender skin. Combined with a black Burberry coat and broad, oxblood, crêpe-soled shoes, it also made me look like some form of being from another planet. Later in life, the infamous Balaclava would become a dependable companion, a trusted friend when taking part in various forms of countryside ramblings or nocturnal sporting pursuits, but for now it was a nuisance and for this trip would be confined to the darkness of my deep coat pocket.

On our journey up the tree-lined back road towards the centre of the town, we must have stopped and listened to every person who crossed our path, reminding me how well my dad was known in these parts. A distance of a couple of miles seemed to be taking as long to complete as a lengthy trek over the steep Cheviot Hills.

Turning into what looked like a large estate, avenues of high-terraced houses towered above us. Every building possessed its own small front garden, surrounded by a low, red brick wall with a privet hedge cosily tucked behind. The hedges looked drab, bare and lifeless at that time of year, as though asleep with their eyelids tightly closed. We passed one garden, where, amid the denser, lower branches of the privet, lay the remains of a nest.

'Look, Dad, a blackie's nest!' He glanced into the depths of the bush.

'Yes, Willie lad, that's definitely a blackie's. Come on now, hurry up! Just around the corner.' I had identified it as the redundant home of Mr and Mrs Blackbird, because of its untidy exterior decor, wrapped with a page from the local weekly tabloid and pieces of clear cellophane. Who taught these birds that paper is a good insulator, I wondered.

Eventually, we arrived at a house where the hedge was taller and untidier than its neighbours'. We paused at the opening: there was a small, wooden gate hanging to one side, only the rusty top hinge stopped it from falling over completely. I was ushered in gently and we walked up the alley, where, at the end, a very tall, secure-looking, black gate stood firmly locked, with a halo of barbed wire wrapped around its head. While peeping through a gap between gate and house, Dad shouted loudly,

'Jimmy, Jimmy! Are you there?' I heard the sound of a door opening hastily.

'Aye, John, I'm coming. Just give me a minute.' A bolt was slid along stiffly at the bottom of the gate, and then another nearer the top. With a rusty creak the gate slowly opened.

Jimmy stared through the narrow slit, sniffing the air like a buck-rat emerging from its hole. He checked behind us inquisitively, making sure the coast was clear before he beckoned us to enter.

Jimmy didn't come across quite the same as I had remembered him. His hair was somewhat tidier, plastered down, greasy and shiny. He wore a chequered shirt, and a red, Paisley-type patterned cravat wrapped loosely around his slender, turkey-like neck. His posture also took on a different guise, not as stooped, although he still appeared very small in comparison to the athletic figure of my dad.

'Come to see my birds, have you?' he asked eagerly. 'Come on in. I'll get the wife to make us a pot of tea.' The tone of his voice implied he was very pleased to see us.

We entered his home by a green, half-panelled door that led directly into the small scullery, where my attention was immediately drawn to the back wall. Three wire cages hung at different levels against a background of eau de Nil. In each cage, a bird jumped livelily between the perches. These songsters took turns to pour out their beautiful melodies, as bacon sizzled in the frying-pan below. Jimmy smiled endearingly, as he watched me observing his birds.

'Like them, eh? Do you know what they are?' I detected an air of arrogance in his question.

'Brown linnets.'

'That's right. The lad certainly knows his birds, John,' he said, glancing towards my dad. Jimmy scuttled over to the frying-pan, got hold of the handle and shook the streaky rashers vigorously.

'Do you know, them linnets always sing when the bacon's frying? Don't know if it's the noise or the smell.' He looked across to my dad and they both laughed. I must admit the aroma of that bacon, which could have shaken off the deepest slumber, was magnificent – a unique blend of good curing and what pigs were fed on in those days.

As we drank our tea and ate our sandwiches – so thick I could hardly get my mouth around them – I could hear birds singing outside. Canaries, mainly, but I also detected the sweet, tinkling song of goldfinches. Our host caught me straining my neck to see out of the window.

'Come on, then. I'll show you what I've got in the shed.' Jimmy got up proudly from his chair and ambled to a nail in the wall on which hung a big, black key. He removed the key from its place, and we all ventured outside, my dad with his half-supped cup of tea, I with the remains of my sandwich.

Walking down the garden path, we passed a cage hanging on the side of the brick outbuilding. In it was another linnet, but this was no ordinary confinement. The bird sat sadly in a lower, wired-off section; above it was an empty compartment. The cage top was raised up at an angle, resembling a lid. I couldn't go past this contraption without first finding out what it was.

'What's that Jimmy?' I asked, pointing to the cage. The old man turned.

'That's one of my drop-in trap cages, for catching some of my birds.' He put his fingers inside and touched a small platform on which lay a sprig of brown, seeded dock. The lid dropped with a metallic click, as Jimmy quickly pulled his fingers out of its way. Then, with a surgical manoeuvre, he carefully reset the lid back in its original, open position, using a straight piece of wire which held the platform in place. He smacked his brown hand firmly down on my shoulder.

'There now, that's how to catch birds with a drop-in trap cage.'

I studied the bird for a few seconds, as Dad and Jimmy strolled towards the shed. It was now frantically banging itself off the sides of its temporary quarters, stressed by the close encounter with Jimmy's hand. I moved a step backwards; almost immediately, it began to settle and gave a long, drawn-out, plaintive, but almost dreamy call. Running to catch up, I called out,

'Do you ever catch any birds here in the garden?' Jimmy turned in my direction, his eyebrows lowered at the doubting tone in my question.

'All the time, lad, all the time.'

The old, stiff lock clicked loudly, as Jimmy turned the key and pushed the door of the shed with his shoulder at the same time. Dad stooped as he entered. This shed was designed to fit its owner, not visitors, wanted or otherwise. Our host guided us inside and then closed the flimsy, wire-netting, safety door behind us. I was here at last, the place of countless recent dreams and wonderings: Jimmy Miller's birdshed.

For me, this place had a feel about it, the sort that causes hairs to rise on the back of your neck. It was cold but not damp, airy but not draughty. Its pungent smell comprised pigeon-loft, hen-house and a hint of wood preserver. It was far from being an unpleasant odour, more— just unusual. All my instincts indicated that this was my type of place, and my eyes scanned every inch of the building's interior, cobwebs and all.

The long back wall boasted banks of fitted cages three tiers high, all roughly the same size. The front bars of these were black, and the inside walls were painted glossy blue-green. On the front of each cage hung a sloping-topped seed-hopper and a half-round, glass water-feeder. Birds would have to put their heads through round holes constructed in the wire to consume their dietary requirements from these receptacles. The cage floors were covered with a mixture of sawdust, sand and peat.

At the far end of the shed was an indoor flight where birds were flying back and forth. I was intrigued, as from this distance I couldn't quite make out what species they were. Jimmy and Dad took a seat on a bench covered in loose-patterned, comfortable-looking cushions, while I began my catwalk, scanning the contents of the cages slowly with eager, excited eyes. Never had I seen such numbers of birds in close proximity. Cage after cage housed goldfinches and linnets. Each one was active, tight-feathered and sleek-looking – a condition synonymous with birds in the peak of health. Behind me, I heard Jimmy's questioning voice.

'See anything you like?' My eyes never left the gems that attracted me so much, as I replied,

'Everything.'

It took me a while to reach the end of the long cage block, pondering over bird after bird of the highest quality. I eventually reached the bottom of the shed, where at last I had an opportunity to analyse the birds in the flight. I was a little anxious at first to ask what they were – I didn't want to show my ignorance, but I had to know.

'What are them birds, Jimmy?' The old man arose from the comfort of his seat, stuck his chest out like a courting pigeon and scurried towards me.

'Those are mule-birds. Some are crosses between goldies and canaries, and others are linnets crossed with canaries.' I cast my critical eye over them, like an expert acquainting himself with a masterpiece hanging on a museum wall. An arrogant grin grew slowly over Jimmy's face.

'Bet you've never seen any of those little beggars before,'

and the grin blossomed into a full-blown smile, revealing his lack of a full complement of teeth, which reminded me that I was to help Dad repair our garden fence when we got home. I had to tell him the truth.

'No, I've never heard of, let alone seen, mule-birds before today. Jimmy, are those the only finches you can cross with canaries for mules?' I asked. The old man returned to his seat and, like the expert he was, began to explain.

'Everything but bullfinch and chaffinch cocks will take a mate that is not of their own kith or kin, but bullie hens have been known to mate successfully with good, big yellow canary cocks and various finch males.' My eyes stole another look at the crossbred birds, vivaciously playing in the flight. These held an instant fascination for me, a lure that was to remain with me for the rest of my life.

Eventually, I dragged myself away from the attraction of the mules and bent down to look at what was on offer in some of the lower cages. These housed canaries, all the same colour – the most exquisite shade of yellow. The nearest colour in comparison was the flowers of the gorse that grew out of control down by the River Blyth and provided five-star accommodation for many breeding pairs of linnets and sanctuary for bashful rabbits or a sly fox. Some cock canaries were singing, but not in the full-throated way they would have if the breeding season had been further on. Other groups of males were bickering, working off a premature spring ardour. Jimmy broke away temporarily from conversation with my dad.

'Those are all cock canaries in there, them in the next block are hens.' I studied these friendly, domesticated birds long and hard, before eventually going to sit with my elders on the bench. The seat was high, and I sat with my bare legs swaying to and fro, as I took in every snippet of information Jimmy's croaky voice offered. When I managed to find a gap in his monologue, I asked my mentor,

'How do you breed those mules?'

'Ah! Now that's a secret, lad. Not many people have the knack of breeding those little mongrels. Gipsy folk would cut yer eyes out for a good goldie mule singing pure goldfinch song. The only misgiving with hybrid birds is you can't breed with them. God may have blessed them with a beauty that can captivate the roughest of men, and a wonderful song to enchant the most sensitive ear, but in his wisdom he wouldn't allow them to beget their own kind. Do you want to hear one sing?'

'Oh! Yes, please!' and I glanced towards Dad for his seal of approval. On seeing this, Jimmy chattered,

'Never mind him. I'm the boss in this hut. Isn't that right, John?' My dad just smiled and nodded.

Jimmy got up, opened the flight door and, with an expertly-controlled swipe picked a goldfinch mule off the small-meshed wire front. With the bird securely in his grip, he lifted an empty wire cage from the wall above the window. He tipped out the old seed and husks onto the floor, blew off the dust-saturated cobwebs and put the bird inside. He proudly placed the cage almost touching my face.

'Beauty, isn't he?' I gazed in amazement at the bird. I had never seen anything like it. Jimmy took the cage outside and hung it on a nail protruding from the side of the shed. He was just starting to walk away from it, when the bird began to sing, and by Christ! did it serenade us. I attempted to show my powers of observation.

'That's a goldfinch's song.'

'Aye, son, as near to pure goldie as you will ever hear in

your lifetime, coming from the beak of a mule. You can learn mules any song you like, but if it's a goldfinch mule, he should have a goldfinch's song; if it's a linnet mule, it should have the song of a linnet – that's my belief.'

My inquisitive nature was now running rampant and overcame any apprehension.

'Jimmy, do you catch all your birds in the garden?'

'Not all of them.' He came towards me and, with a Fagan-like tap on his nose, said,

'I gets a lot of them a bit further afield, from my secret places.' I stood back slightly.

'Do you always use those drop-in traps like the one on the wall?'

'Not all the time. Sometimes, I use run-in traps, flap nets or the wands and bird-lime.'

I switched my gaze to a goldfinch in one of the cages and then turned back with a questioning grimace on my face.

'Jimmy, what are wands and bird-lime?' He stood motionless for a moment.

'Here, lift up.' Dad and I stood awkwardly, as he raised the top part of the seat to expose an array of traps and nets. He plunged his hand blindly into the box, in the same way I would pick out a thruppenny lucky-dip from the cardboard box in old Mrs McPeak's corner shop at the end of our street. His hand emerged with a small tubular container. The seat cover closed with a dusty bang, and we all sat back down again.

'These are wands.'

From the metal tube, he removed around 20 long, thin sticks, each one split at one end, with the tips of the split shaped to an angle, rather like a 'V'. Fine, dark thread was wrapped and bound tightly in the middle of the split, to about an inch up the shaft. These sticks were covered in a sticky substance – bird-lime. He pulled approximately half the sticks away from the rest. Then, after circling the two lots around each other a number of times, he pulled them apart. I could see how tacky they were by the way he separated them stiffly.

'You puts these where the birds you want to catch are feeding, on thistle tops, burdock or seeded chickweed, or even on the callbird's cage. You hide close to hand, and when the bird comes down, it gets caught on the sticks.' He thrust the bunch of wands right into my face.

'You counts the number of wands you put down, and you picks the same number up when yer finished. Never, never leave any behind.' For a moment, I saw anger as hot as hell's fire smouldering in Jimmy's squinting eyes.

'Never set wands and leave them. Stay in sight of them till yer done,' he ordered. Here endeth the lesson, I thought to myself.

On seeing the angry side of Jimmy's character for the first time, I thought I'd better change the subject for a moment, so he could cool down a bit.

'Jimmy, what's the best for catching?'

'It all depends, Billy lad. For bullfinches and goldfinches, I say the drop-in trap, for linnets and greenfinches it's the run-in type trap, for redpolls you can use anything – those little beggars will go into paper bags or empty cans. I've seen redpolls waiting impatiently at a closed trap for you to open the door so they could get in.' For a moment I didn't know whether he was joking or not, but when I spotted the sly wink between him and Dad, I realised he was being facetious.

It seemed as though he was slowly entering the mode of a parson, preaching from his pulpit to the gathered congregation.

'If birds are in flocks, feeding on the September stubble,

there's only one on – the flap net. You can catch a hell of a lot of birds in the right place, especially those that are inclined to flock up: linnets, greenies, chaffinches and the likes.' Here we go, I thought to myself, this will put the weasel among the canaries.

'What about the wands?' His face winced as though he was suffering an agonising death.

'I only use them as a last resort. Those things can be killers. They are cruel and they will eventually land the person who uses them in hot water. Stick to nets and trap cages, lad.' Not being the sort of person, even at that tender age, to give up, I tempted fate with more cross-examination.

'Jimmy, how do you make bird-lime?' His stack was well and truly blown now.

'Forget the wands! Look here,' and he took two traps from the wall, a drop-in cage and a run-in type, both well constructed and painted glossy black. From the side of our seat, he pulled out a rolled-up hessian bag – a 'poke' as we call them in North-umberland. He deposited the two cages into the sack and passed it to me.

'Don't let anyone see what you have in there. Can the lad have a goldie cock for his bedroom, John?' Before my dad could answer, I was excitedly shouting,

'Yes, Dad! Please, Dad!' My father never acknowledged my pleadings, as he turned and explained to Jimmy,

'No, we've got nowhere to put one, and there's no way his mother will let one in the house. One day, I will fix a shed up, and he'll get one off you.' In my mind, I threw every curse I could think of at him for not allowing me to have a bird. Look-ing back, however, it would have been a silly thing to do. The proper time would eventually come and, when it did, there would be no greater colleague than my father to help and en-courage my interests in aviculture.

Over an hour had elapsed since our arrival, and Dad got up, signalling that it was time to leave.

'Come on then, Willie. Better be getting back – see what your mother's burning for the dinner.' I didn't want to go; I could have stayed there forever: I had quickly become a member of the Jimmy the Ragman fan club. I picked up my bag of freebies at a snail's pace, employing similar delaying tactics as much as I could, and took one last look at the birds.

'Bye then, Jimmy. I have to go,' I said, gingerly. He placed his hand gently on my arm and spoke almost apologetically.

'Right, lad. Don't forget where I live; and don't wait for old frosty face there to bring you next time. If you're good, I will take you out trapping one morning.' My head lifted instantly, chasing away any gremlins of disappointment. This was an offer I couldn't believe, nor refuse – it spurred me not to put a foot wrong for many weeks. My inborn love of and interest in birds was strong, and I also felt – at that time – as though the idea of catching the birds I worshipped was a part of me, a natural thing to do. Jimmy was just the lighter of the blue touch-paper that would rocket me into the secretive and, in some cases, solitary world of trapping birds.

I left Jimmy's abode and the gentle hospitality of his wife, and returned home to thoughts and dreams of what was to come – and what times there were! Not just trapping birds, but also getting myself into positions that would bring me closer to the wildlife I was interested in and loved so much.

I found it difficult to sleep that evening, eventually slipping into the abyss of dreamy slumber with images of long, ivory-beaked goldfinches and linnets dressed in crimson waistcoats flashing through my head. What a day it had been! An experience which lives with me today as clearly as it did all those years ago.

CHAPTER 3

THE PEACHY CATCHER

My 11th birthday at the end of January had come in like a lion and gone out like a lamb – I was lucky the way my parents, grandparents and some favourite aunties celebrated my birthdays, always making me feel I was the most loved and most wanted person in the whole world. But now, after all the hard frosts, snow, driving rain and biting cold winds, it was February, the month that derives its name from *februa*, the Roman festival of purification.

On a dull Saturday morning at the beginning of the month, I was out of bed early. The plan was to explore the fields and hedgerows along the banks of the nearby River Blyth, towards the Halfpenny Woods. Friends and I had arranged to meet on the playing-field close to my home. It was getting late – the chiming bells of St John's Church warned me it was nine o'clock. My pals were still nowhere in sight, so I left. I was that type of boy, never afraid of being alone out in the countryside, exploring mother nature's wonders. In fact, I secretly relished the idea.

As I sauntered up the back lane, I was greeted by old Mrs Purdy's dog, Duke. This animal possessed the uncanny knack of appearing from nowhere, as plans were being prepared for bird-nesting, rabbit or rat-hunting expeditions. He would regularly accompany my friends and me with all the loyalty of a Ghurkha but, on returning home, he would disappear as quickly as a startled rabbit. Like us, he lived for roaming the

23

fields in search of adventure, but I doubt if his real owner ever realised the true hunting nature of her pet, as she sat in front of her warm fire, staring dozily at the blue, purple, orange and red flames dancing their silent jig of peace and tranquillity.

Duke was of unknown pedigree. He stood 24 inches at the shoulder and was raven black with a thin white flash on his chest. His head gave the impression he possessed Labrador in his genetic make-up, but otherwise his physical characteristics yelled out greyhound. His thick-feathered tail turned up completely, almost forming a circle as it just about touched his back. Aesthetically, he would never have won a canine beauty contest, but this backstreet cur was the best killer of rats I had ever seen.

'Come on then, Duke! Let's see what we can find on this fine morning.' His head immediately cocked to one side, as he detected the thrill and excitement in the tone of my voice: his ears pinned back and gripped his head, the curly tail wagged stiffly, and his big, lustrous eyes resembled those of a cat preparing to pounce. At times, I am sure our canine companions understand more than we give them credit for.

The early part of our morning's quest took us along railway embankments raised up between the seaport of Blyth and Ashington, once reputed to be the largest mining town in the country. The grey, aggregate-covered sides were steep and sloped down to a broken fence that was partly covered with pale green lichens. Staggered along these banks, bushes of willow, alder and elder had taken up residence. Tall grasses, as well as greater stitchwort, ragwort, meadowsweet and stinging nettle, grew naturally in gaps between the scrub. At that time of the year, the undergrowth was sparse – a far cry from the vibrant, replenishing summer months when this untamed garden would be transformed into an impenetrable jungle – an ideal breeding-ground for willow warblers, whitethroats, robin and wren; with foraging stoats and darting weasels roaming on the dense, grass-covered floor sponged with moss, while shy wood mice and pygmy shrews lived a life of hiding from these fearless hunters. Lying tired and low to the ground, the searching green fingers of brambles also occupied this setting; and hundreds of plate-pies, tarts and puddings boiled in clouts would have been made from collected blackberries during the autumn months, and numerous families of white-rumped bullfinches would have gorged themselves on the tender, ebony fruit.

Suddenly, the ever-alert Duke drove into the thicket with a total disregard for the ripping actions of the plant's sharp thorns. I shouted loudly, encouraging the dog to chase.

'Go on, Duke! Get in there!' The dog zig-zagged at high speed in hot pursuit of a prey that, for the moment, was invisible to him, and whose only trace was the trail of sweet scent it had unwittingly left behind. My keen eyes switched instantly from the bushes on which they had been focused and, in the distance, I saw the fleeting, grey outline of a rabbit nipping across the path and disappearing through the fence surrounding the Grammar School playing-fields. A moment later, Duke emerged from the bushes, his head swishing from side to side as he changed his olfactory powers over to those of sight, searching for the creature that had eluded him. He crossed the path and stood with his nose pushed between the triangular-shaped wooden rails, with a look on his face that seemed to ask, Where the hell did it go?

The dog was unsuccessful on this occasion, but there would be many other instances when victory would be attained, and I would return home proudly with a rabbit for my dad's supper.

Out of the corner of my eye, I caught sight of the dark figure of a man entering bushes at the bottom of the lane, just past the entrance to the Old Park. The shrubbery there was thicker, mainly talon-clad branches of hawthorn and blackthorn. Making in that general direction, I couldn't help thinking to myself, He's up to no good. My canine hunting companion once again explored the depths of the brambles, wending his way through, searching frenziedly for more scents. I carried on at a quite leisurely pace, when a handsome male blackbird flew from the bushes and landed on the path. He looked up at me with big, yellow-rimmed eyes, his head cocked to one side, as though asking, Who are you? His large, fanned tail dipped a number of times before he lifted, flying off low to the ground, screeching out an alarm call at the same time.

I arrived approximately where the sly looking figure had entered the bushes and peered cautiously in. To break the silence, I called for the dog.

'Duke, Duke!'

The sound of crashing twigs burst from the undergrowth. Then, from the shadows emerged a man – it was Jimmy Miller. A mask of panic adorned his face.

'Get yer dog! Ave got a trap set.' Then, on realising who I was, he summoned,

'Oh! It's you, youngin. Get yer dog quickly and come in here.' Duke surfaced from the bushes with the hackles on his neck standing as stiff as a council road-sweeper's brush. Although friendly to my friends and me, he was always very leery in the presence of strangers. I grabbed the grumbling dog by the scruff and trailed Jimmy into the bushes.

A short distance in, Jimmy sat down next to the twisted, shiny brown trunk of a hawthorn that grew at an angle, as though to make a natural, high-backed throne for him. I squatted humbly beside him on the twig-covered ground. At his feet were two wire-fronted wooden boxes. Jimmy was staring attentively towards the railway embankment and pointed.

'Over there, lad, there's my trap cage. Can you see it?' I could just make out the black wires of a cage, positioned between two clumps of tall grass.

'What are you after, Jimmy?'

'Peachies,' he replied and, lifting one of the boxes, he allowed me to inspect its contents. I looked closely through the wire and saw a moving mass of red-breasted, fluttering lesser redpolls.

I was surprised at so many birds being crammed into such a small box.

'Jimmy, how many is in there?'

'Lost count, lad. They were coming thick and fast earlier. Quiet! I think I can hear some more coming.' We looked skywards through a gap in the bush's upper branches. I too heard the *tew, tew, tew* of redpolls in the distance. I could also hear the redpoll in Jimmy's trap cage, a callbird used to lure the wildlings, like the mythical Sirens, who called sailors to their doom on rocks in shallow waters.

We sat motionless as two diminutive birds came dipping into view from the grey sky and landed close to the trap cage. My arm tightened around the dog's thick neck. Duke's dark eyes too were trained in the direction of the trap cage, as an intense feeling of excitement flooded our hiding-place. The three of us watched as the redpolls feasted on the seeds of the silky bent-grass partly hiding the cage. This trap wasn't the

same design as the one I had studied on my maiden visit to Jimmy's garden. The callbird was in a central compartment, and there were two traps, one either side of the bird. Both traps were the same drop-in type. Their spring-loaded lids were in the open position.

Within minutes one of the redpolls flew down and landed on the side of the trap cage, trilling energetically, as though challenging the callbird below him. A split second later and with no hesitation, it dropped in. Got it, I thought to myself, and nearly jumped up from my seat. Jimmy must have sensed my intention, and his arm came up across my chest to stop me – he said nothing. The second redpoll, spooked by the noise of the trap, flew up and landed on a swaying branch directly above us. My heart was pounding with excitement, but I dared not move a neck muscle to see it. My eyeballs strained painfully sideways in an attempt to locate its exact position, but only a continuous twittering and trilling let us know it was still there. What seemed like an eternity passed before this bird too flew down and landed on the cage. Around the top of the closed trap it clambered, with the actions of a blue tit raiding a bag of nuts. A little flutter and it was on the edge of the open trap. I was now cross-fingered, willing it to alight on the trap's activating treadle. Again, with no messing around, this bird took the bait and dropped in. Jimmy turned, at the same time pointing like a gunner sending his spaniel to bring the quarry back to its master.

'Now, go and get the cage, lad.'

I scrambled on all fours towards the trap; Jimmy grabbed the dog as it tried to follow me. Caught in the cage were two lovely lesser redpolls, with rich red on their breasts and rumps, and dark crimson caps on their heads. I returned with the cage and in went Jimmy's thin hand, taking each bird in turn out of the traps. The birds were inspected: he held them by the tips of their wings and tail, nipped between his fore-finger and thumb. I had never seen a bird held in this way before. He presented the bird in front of me.

'Nice un, eh?' Then he put it with the birds he had caught earlier, in one of the wire-fronted boxes he called his 'stow boxes'.

Jimmy spoke with a sigh.

'There now, I think that's enough for this morning. Do you fancy coming up to my place?' I must admit I would have preferred to stay a while longer, but I agreed to accompany him. He pulled a rolled-up poke from inside his jacket.

'We'll put the stow boxes in here, and I will hide the trap cage.' Rather than carry the bulky trap home, it was carefully hidden in the undergrowth, as a sly fox would conceal his larder just under the soil and covered with grass, moss and fallen leaves. When he did need to take it home, he would return to collect it once the cloak of darkness concealed his presence. He turned and, in a commanding voice, ordered,

'Don't tell yer mates where this is, lad.'

As though I would have!

We headed off with our bags of swag to Jimmy's house. Duke, however, pictured other things in his mind and made off in the opposite direction. I called to him – his tail waved an acknowledging wag – but when this dog considered there was no excitement left for him, he would put on his deaf head and nothing would change his mind. See ya later then, Duke, I thought to myself, and turned to follow the bow-legged fig-ure steaming away in front of me.

When we eventually arrived at Jimmy's house, we by-passed any welcomes and went directly to his shed. Once in-side, he opened the door to one of the cages, lifted the side of one of the stow boxes containing the newly-caught redpolls and put the open end level with the cage door. He flicked the box a couple of times with his finger, chasing all the birds into their new, temporary accommodation. The second box was also emptied this way. Jimmy's voice altered noticeably to a pleading tone.

'There now, can you count them for me?' I squeezed past him and began to tally up the fluttering birds while he poured water into a shallow earthenware dish, swilled it around, then emptied the contents into an algae-lined metal bucket in the corner of the shed. As he filled the dish a second time, he explained,

'Some trapped birds sulk and can't find their water, so it is best to place the container inside the cage for the first few days.' A number of the redpolls were on the floor of their new enclosure; some clung onto the front bars, while others sat nervously on the perches. I watched closely as one by one the newly-caughts began to crack open seeds placed in the cage for them. I eventually managed to count them without falling asleep and called to Jimmy.

'Twenty-two.'

At first, he gave the impression he wasn't too excited at the size of his catch.

'Not bad, not bad at all.' Then, like a man possessed, he sprung up, and I half expected him to shout *eureka!* He smacked his hands together and, with a beaming smile, asked,

'Who's the best peachy catcher in Northumberland?' I laughed, not so much at the question, more at the old fool's morris-dancing antics.

'You are, Jimmy, you are!'

CHAPTER 4

A BULGING NET

It was mid-February. The countryside was locked securely in dark, drab dampness. In this situation, most people would be as miserable as the weather itself, but I was looking forward to the coming weekend with eagerness. A bird-trapping expedition with my old ragman friend into places where push and rush are forbidden was in the offing.

Jimmy and I were quickly forming a bond, and I visited him on every possible occasion. I regularly swapped the stuffy school classroom for the tonic of his beckoning shed, learning from my surrogate teacher, while observing the birds I loved so much. Jimmy's eldest son, Dicky, was the same way inclined as his father – a trapper, a poacher and a night-time skulker – but he was now branching into the scholarship of beer and the beauty of the female form, so venturing out on a cold and frosty morning trapping birds was low on his list of priorities. Alan, Jimmy's middle son, was a great lad and a very good school friend of mine, but he possessed no interest whatsoever in birds or the ways of the countryside.

On the Saturday afternoon, I visited Jimmy to help with his birds and finalise strategies for the next day. The tall gate to his back garden was locked as usual. I knocked on the front door and was greeted by the friendly, smiling face of his wife.

'Come in, Billy. Just go through – he's in the birdshed.'

She led me into the cosy sitting-room, through the linnet-filled kitchen and into the garden. While I was wandering down the garden path, Jimmy's face appeared goblin-like at the discoloured window of the shed. His eyes squinted as though he couldn't make out who was approaching. Then his hand went up and he opened the sturdy door.

Once I was in and seated, Jimmy asked,

'Been anywhere nice?'

'Not really, but I came up by the Old Park and saw a load of bullfinches.'

'Bullies, eh? We might have a look down there some-time.' My ears pricked.

'Tomorrow?'

'No, lad. Bullies will be feeding on buds now and, once they do, you stand no chance of enticing them down to the cage.' I paused for a moment.

'So when will we be able to go out for some?' Jimmy looked me right in the eye.

'Now take this in – it might be the best piece of information I will be giving you today: the times for catching bullies are July and August, when the young ones are on the go, or back end of the year, when the frosts and cold weather come. The harder the weather, the better for getting them big buggers.'

With this useful piece of information permanently stored in the filing cabinet of my head, I began to look through the cages to see whether there were any new additions to Jimmy's illicit avian collection. That was one of the many excitements in going to Jimmy's place: you could visit one day and see what was on offer, come back a few days later and find an array of new birds there. Where he got them all from was a mystery to me at that time.

Jimmy picked up a small, wooden-handled brush and began sweeping seed husks off the worn, lino-covered floor. Without looking up, he said,

'Take a good look around, youngin. Got some new birds in for you to see.' My eyes searched deeper into the room, pin-pointing an interesting, all-wire cage hanging on the far wall. In it was the best goldfinch cock I'd ever seen – so big, so resplendently coloured. I gasped.

'Where on earth did you get him from, Jimmy?' The old man got up, the knees of his brown, corduroy trousers covered in chaff and dust.

'Beauty, isn't he? I thought you would like that 'n. It's a spink that is, lad, a definite spink.' A puzzled expression took temporary residence on my face.

'What's a spink, Jimmy?' Flushed with success at making me ponder, he adopted a school master's stance.

'Well, lad, take yer eyes off him for a minute, sits down, and old Jimmy will tell you. Most goldies in these parts are *knoppers* – small, dark-coloured birds with black legs; but occasionally you get these bigger, brighter-coloured birds with white legs – *spinks* we call them.' I glanced back at the goldfinch in the cage; the bird did fit Jimmy's description. With his eyes popping, and his claw-like hand gripping my arm, Jimmy exclaimed,

'I've been offered £4 for him!' Now, this sum was a fair amount in those days, especially for a bird.

'Are you going to take it?'

'Thinking about it, lad, thinking about it.'

I quickly browsed through the remaining cages, where I found some other additions since my last visit. These new acquisitions included more goldfinches and some linnet cocks. I also noticed there were fewer redpolls in the shed.

'Where's all the peachies, Jimmy?'

'Gave some to a bloke from Lynemouth, and little Selby Hills got a couple – they've always been Selby's favourites.'

'Jimmy, are you the best bird-catcher in Northumberland?'

'I wish I was, lad. There are some good trappers in this neck of the woods – not just trappers, great birdmen. I could be the best in Bedlington though.' Now, there was a statement for my animated mind to contend with.

'Who else in Bedlington catches?' He threw his head back and laughed.

'Tell you the truth, I can't think of anybody.

'Here's a one for you, lad. How do you accurately sex goldfinches?' Now this stopped me in my tracks. Smugly, I looked at him, checking his face for give away signs of this being a trick question.

'That's easy. If the blaze† goes past the eye, it's a male; if it doesn't, it's a hen.' Jimmy stretched up and removed a wire cage containing a goldfinch from the wall above the shed window.

'So what's this?' I cast my expert eye over the bird.

'Hen.'

This awoke the thick, hairy, caterpillar-like eyebrows on Jimmy's forehead. A smirk bloomed into life on his wrinkled face, and I began to doubt the accuracy of my response.

'Better look again, your lordship. Get the bird out the cage – that's the first rule. Never make your mind up from first impressions.'

Doing as I was bid, I took the bird in my hand and gave the area around its eye a closer examination. The rich vermilion colour extended halfway through the eye.

† the red patch on the front of a goldfinch's head.

'Yes, it's a hen, definitely a hen.' Jimmy peered with one eye half-closed, as though trying to get to my very soul.

'Well, now, how do you account for this goldie being the father to the mule-birds in the bottom flight?' It was his turn to be smug. 'Like I said to you before, lad, don't make judgements on your first impressions. Believe half what folk tell you, and three quarters of what they show you. Now, give me the bird.' I carefully handed over the goldfinch in the way I had been taught, making sure it was in his grasp, before I let go of my own gentle, but sure, hold.

'Now, look and listen. Jimmy will teach you how to sex a goldfinch. When you checked the bird, all you looked at was its blaze. In some cases, this works, especially if the red goes well past the eye. The trouble with this is when a male is a poor-coloured specimen, or when a hen possesses an exceptionally good colour, or if she's an older bird. Accurate sexing takes a number of details of the bird into account.'

Moving the bird expertly through his fingers, he told me, 'The physical size of a male is usually larger than a female's. The spike† of a cockbird is also noticeably bigger than that of a hen. Next tell-tale sign: the colour on the top of its head. On a hen, this black is mottled with brown, or some-times grey. A cock's is as black as tar. This also applies to the black coloration on the wings' butts.

'Now, take the bird again and tell me, what colour are the small, fine hairs just above the bird's beak?' Like a jewel-ler checking a rare diamond, I examined the bird in hand.

'Black,' I answered. Jimmy wagged his pointed finger.

'There now, that's another sign for you to jot down in that little book you keep at home – the same hairs on a hen would be much lighter.' Once again, he took the bird from

† the beak

37

me and returned it to its cage, at the same time saying, 'Even greypates† can be sexed by the colour of these hairs.'

Hanging the cage back on the same nail above the window where it came from, he asked,

'Do you think you will be able to sex goldfinches accurately in the future?'

'Yes, Jimmy, I'll never make a mistake again.'

'Do you really think so? I still get the odd one wrong and I've kept birds all my life.'

At times like this, Jimmy's enthusiasm unfolded like a painted fan, but at other times he was hard work, needing to be prompted and prodded for information.

A glass drinker on one of the cages was nearly empty; I picked up a bottle of fresh water from the floor and filled it till it overflowed.

'Where are we going tomorrow, Jimmy?'

'Never mind. Just be here for five o'clock.'

'Five! It's still dark then,' I exclaimed.

'Yes, and it's bloody cold too. Look, just say if you don't want to come.'

'I'll be here. Don't worry.'

'I'm not worried. If you're not here, I will bloody go without you.' He sounded as though he wasn't bothered whether I turned up or not, but I think he was.

The next morning, I was woken by our old clock blasting out its angry alarm. Ferret-like, I stuck my nose out from under the covers, but it was freezing. At this point, I was in two minds whether to get up or not. The pink, rubber, hot-water bottle that had been such a warm companion a few hours earlier was now like a block of ice, and I kicked and pushed it aggressively to the foot of the bed. It took all my discipline

† pre-first-moult goldfinches

finally to shove the bedclothes back and leave the warmth and sanctuary of my lair. I scraped ice from the inside of the bedroom window with my fingernails to look outside. At first, I thought snow was lying on the garden, but on closer inspection I saw it was frost, a very hard frost, sparkling and glistening like an illuminated Christmas card. I got dressed, putting on two of every item of clothing. When fully clad, I headed off like Scott on an Antarctic expedition.

As I entered Jimmy's street, I could make out a warm, tender glow coming from his house, like a ship's lamp twinkling in a secluded bay. I was slowly getting acclimatised to the hostile weather and, for the moment, the cold no longer held me captive. I was, however, aware of a feeling of excitement starting to flow through my body. I enjoyed this, the sensation of being alone, in the dark, with no one else about.

I arrived at my destination, and Jimmy let me in through the front door.

'There's a pot of tea waiting for you on the kitchen table, lad. Get it into you – we're going nowhere till we've drunk our brew.'

'What if I hadn't of come?'

'I knew you would be here. I knew you wouldn't let old Jimmy down.' I dared not tell him how much it was touch and go when I first awoke and felt the lick of Jack Frost's icy tongue across the tip of my nose.

Drinking my tea, I watched Jimmy arranging a number of cages and wooden stow boxes. He lifted a wire cage down off the kitchen wall and passed it over.

'Get that linnet and put it in the smallest wire cage.' When he said small cage, he certainly meant small – it literally fitted in the palm of my hand.

'Will it be all right in there?'

'Of course. It's only his home for a couple of hours.' I switched the bird, and now it became apparent what we were going for.

With the bird secure in the cage, I stood ready and in anticipation of my next given task. Jimmy was scurrying mouse-like around the kitchen.

'Put those four stow boxes into the haversack.' It was his son, Alan's, bag; I recognised it from football training.

'Four stow boxes?'

'Yes, if everything goes well, we might fill the lot,' he replied.

'Time to go. Get the haversack,' Jimmy ordered in sergeant-major fashion. He picked up a fishing-rod in its cover and another haversack already packed and securely fastened. The small cage containing the linnet was placed inside his coat. Closing the door to the house quietly behind us, we set off.

We were wrapped in the cloak of darkness as we wended our way through the streets, lanes and then well-trodden pathways down towards the riverside.

'We're nearly safe now.' He was pointing towards high bushes and trees silhouetted against a sky that was slowly changing from black to dark violet. The heavens were cloudless and stars were still clearly visible. The Plough and the Pole Star stared down at us, and a long-tailed shooting star arced across our path.

I must admit I always felt more comfortable when among the trees and bushes of the countryside, as opposed to the concrete and clay of streets and buildings. If you're participating in some form of illicit enterprise, there are no better hiding-places than in the gardens of mother nature.

'How far are we going?' I asked.

'Down the fields towards the Granary Point.' This was a piece of land separating the River Blyth from the River Sleek. In bygone days, tracks led all the way to the point, and these carried trains laden with grain, iron-ore and other produce to be loaded onto barges and boats berthed there. This post-industrial landscape was now partly taken over by farmland; the rest possessed the glib definition of wasteland, an ideal environment for finch flocks such as linnets.

We trekked along a path directly above the winding river-bank. Overgrown branches of gorse and broom draped the way, prickling our legs as we pushed past them. Daylight was breaking in flowing waves. The clattering cry of a startled blackbird echoed in front of us, and I could make out the white, bobbing tail of a rabbit disappearing into the dense grass. Jimmy whispered,

'Right, this is the way we go now,' and we parted company with the well-worn trail. He threw the fishing-rod into the field and unsteadily scaled the three-strung wire fence. I followed closely, dodging his foot as it swung over the top wire. Up the hedge-line we travelled, towards the crest of the field. Looking over the hedge, I could make out an area of uncultivated land.

'This is it, lad. We're here.' We put our bags on the ground close to a small group of bushes higher and denser than those surrounding the area. Gingerly, Jimmy pushed through a small gap in the hedge; I waited for my turn to follow.

'Bring the fishing-rod bag, Billy,' his voice grunting as he crawled badger-like. Once in the field, I followed like a dog as Jimmy paced out a distance from the hedge to a large patch of thistles standing defiantly amid ground plants of chickweed, burdock, groundsel and plantain.

'Twenty-eight, twenty-nine, thirty. This will do here. Pass me the rod bag,' he demanded, at the same time taking the cage containing the linnet out from under his coat. He placed the cage on the grass and began opening the long, green, canvas rod-case.

'Why fetch a fishing-rod?' I asked.

'Two reasons: first, it makes people thinks we are going or have been fishing, not catching birds. Second, it's not exactly a fishing-rod,' and he removed a number of canes from the bag. Placing them on the ground, he began to join them up at the corners using clip-like arrangements taken from his coat pocket. A fine, small-meshed net was removed from a poacher's pocket sewn onto the inside of his heavy-looking coat.

'It's a net!' I proclaimed.

He smirked.

'Yes, it's a clap net. These are the boys for skittling flocks of linnets.' The complete contraption was assembled with masterful precision. The frame of the net was hinged in the middle and jointed by two pieces of strong, quarter-inch-square, black elastic, so that, when it was laid on the ground, half of it would act like a flap.

He positioned the net and pulled it back to what was its loaded position. A piece of thick wire was placed strategically to form a makeshift trigger arrangement.

'You fasten this string to this wire and, when the birds are inside the net, you pulls as hard as you can.' He demonstrated, throwing his arm back as though striking for a trout taking a fly on the end of a fine fishing-line.

'How do you know when to pull?'

'You pulls when I tells you to pull, and not before.'

The bird in the cage was positioned within striking distance of the net's grab, and a bag containing waste seed was emptied around it. Jimmy walked backwards to the hedge, feeding out the string from a small, wooden fishing-reel.

'Pick up all the bits and pieces, lad. Hurry now.' I cleaned up and scurried back to the hedge. One after the other, we crawled through the gap and bedded ourselves down, positioned so we could make out the callbird's cage.

'Is it me, Jimmy, or is it getting colder?'

'Aye, lad, it sometimes happens like this. The morning brings the rest of the cold promised by the night's frost. All the better for our job – the linnets will be panicking about where they're going to get their breakfast.'

We waited, crouching in the undergrowth, talking quietly only when it was necessary. From the direction of the river behind us, the soft piping calls of plovers could be heard. High in the sky, a group of redshanks wheeled around us, banking sharply before descending towards the shimmering mud flats. Their scolding *t-keep, t-keep* alarm call could be heard continuously as they landed gently.

'Look, lad,' said Jimmy, pointing to the sky. I could make out a soft, irregular-shaped blur moving around in a jerking, sweeping manner.

'Linnets. Keep well down. Don't look up – they can spot your white face even from that height. Just watch the cage.' The flock was coming in our direction and, as they got closer, the distinct, dreamy, twittering calls of linnets could be heard. Then the group switched direction a little.

'What's the matter with that damn callbird?' Jimmy's voice was full of anger – he was panicking a little. 'We're going to miss them.' He gave out a few call notes of his own, which mimicked a linnet's remarkably well. On hearing this, the callbird was spurred into his full, varied song.

'That's amazing,' I whispered. The flock, in turn, heard

the Judas callbird. Down, down, down they descended from the sky, bouncing on invisible stepping-stones. Lower and lower they bobbed and jinked in the direction of the net. Finally they came into land, the group splitting into two smaller clusters, the larger one landing approximately 10 yards from the cage, the smaller group a little further from it. We stared motionless as the flock fed and moved, fed and moved, slowly but surely making its way towards the net. Some were hopping, others lifting in dipping flight, dropping closer and closer each time.

It now seemed a large percentage of the group were feeding on the waste seed around the cage. I mimed to Jimmy asking whether I should pull the string. He shook his head and whispered softly,

'No, not yet. Let some more hang themselves first.' More and more birds edged towards the cage. The flock was now feeding frantically with an almost total disregard for their safety. Hunger had, for the moment, removed their inborn defences of being wary and suspicious. Again, I signalled to my mentor, asking whether I should pull the string. Again his head shook. My hands were sweating – I was getting anxious that the flock would be spooked and lift, leaving us with nothing. It looked as though every bird was feeding within the net's grabbing reach.

'Now, Billy! Pull the string!'

I yanked as hard as I could, falling on my backside in the process. Now, pulling a string may sound like an easy task, but oh! how I prayed nothing had gone wrong. Had it worked? Had the string snapped? Had the birds lifted before the net clapped to the frost-hardened ground?

I clambered to my knees and gazed unsurely towards the net, as Jimmy jumped up like a startled hare lifting from its form. He cut through the hedge and into the field. Beyond the running figure, I couldn't see many birds flying off, only a small number to the right of the cage, and a smaller number to the left. I dropped the string from my clammy hand and quickly followed in Jimmy's tracks.

With my youthful zeal, I practically caught Jimmy up before he reached the net. There I saw a sight that will stay imprinted in my memory for the rest of my days. The net was bulging with fluttering, flapping birds. It was so full it was actually inches off the ground. The need to talk in a low voice had gone now, and Jimmy screeched out his orders like Collingwood at the height of a bloody battle with the French Fleet.

'Pin that side! Hold it down!' Jimmy dived to the ground like a rugby prop-forward and ended up kneeling on the frame of the net, holding it down with his hands. 'Keep the edge on the ground. Don't let any escape!'

When we were in total control of the situation, Jimmy bent over the net, his speech distorted by panting breath.

'Go! Go fetch the stow boxes from the bushes. Hurry, lad!' I sprinted, not wanting to be away from the net and the birds inside it for one moment. I returned and emptied the contents of the haversack onto the grass.

'Get a box out, quickly now. Open the door and come here, close to me.' Jimmy squeezed his slender hand under the net among the captured linnets. Out he pulled a single bird.

'Cock,' he said, and put it into the open box I was holding. His hand went in again, another male and another addition to the box. The next time he withdrew a bird, he blew on the feathers of its chest.

'Hen,' he exclaimed, and then, opening his hands, released it. I made a frantic grab as the female linnet flew past me. She threw an exuberant, trilling twitter at us for frightening her.

'Leave it, Billy. The hens are no use to us – we're only keeping the cockbirds.'

This separating out went on for quite a long while: cock in the box, hen let away; cock in the box, hen let away. I must admit I never liked the idea of letting anything away once caught, but we filled four stow boxes with male linnets.

'Kept a count, lad?' Jimmy asked, with a doubtful look on his face.

'Forty-seven.'

'Let one out. I hate odd numbers.'

'You're joking!' It was bad enough letting the hens out, without letting a bloody cockbird out as well, I thought to myself.

'No, lad, I'm very superstitious that way. I hate odd numbers. It's the Romany blood flowing through my veins, you know.' Hesitantly following my master's command, I put my hand into one of the boxes and pulled out the first bird I got hold of. I looked at it, kissed the top of its head and let it go. With a twist on his face that would have taken a major honour at a gurning competition, Jimmy asked,

'What was that for?'

'A kiss for luck. It's the Romany blood flowing through my veins, you know.' Jimmy laughed out loud.

'Stupid little bugger!' at the same time shoving me with a friendly, but firm, push.

After a minute or so, it was time to leave. For a moment, Jimmy's face had concern written all over it.

'Old Joe Binney, the farmer, will be down before long. We

will have five minutes' rest a bit further up in the next field. Better get away from here.' We collected all our belongings, double-checked nothing remained lying in the grass, and left the hospitality of this piece of productive wasteland. We made our way to the other side of the field. A solitary old cow was lying in front of the dry-stone wall, close to the gate. When we were near, Jimmy went over and gave the old girl a hefty kick to shift her.

'There now. A nice warm seat for us.' We sat down for a well-earned rest as the cow strode off, stopped for a moment, turned, and gave us a dirty look for disturbing her rest and stealing her warm mattress.

When we eventually returned to Jimmy's, we emptied the full stow boxes into larger compartments.

'I'll sort them out later,' Jimmy said. 'I bet you're tired now.'

'No, not really,' I said, but I was – very tired indeed. We planned for me to come back later, after some well-deserved sleep.

I ran excitedly all the way home, eager to tell my dad what we had caught. I told him of the cold when I had got up, about the shooting stars, how Jimmy had called the birds down and of the net lifting off the ground full of linnets.

Dad listened intently like the interested, considerate parent he was and, as I paused for a breather, said,

'This bird thing is certainly getting hold of you. We might have to start thinking of getting your own birdshed before long.' I could hardly contain myself.

'Honest, Dad, honest? When can I have one?'

'Soon. I will try and sort one out.' He got up out of his seat and, as he went into the kitchen, turned. 'But for hell's sake don't keep pestering me about it' – regret for the promise in the tone of his voice. This was the icing on the cake. I would never get to sleep now. I grabbed my leather football and kicked the hell out of it against the coal-house wall. I needed to work off my excitement.

I had many more successful outings with old Jimmy. I never got the chance to thank him for teaching me about birds and the ways of the wildlings before he died. In those early days, he trained me in such a way I didn't realise I was being taught. I hope these few early chapters go some way towards thanking him – some short tales of a little man, who loved birds in a big way: the linnet man – Jimmy Miller.

CHAPTER 5

RAFFIE

My keen interest in wildlife can be traced to a very early age: when I was eight years old, my parents were told by my primary school teacher, Miss Waddington, whose wonderful nature (an amazing thing beauty!) endeared her to me so much, 'If we were to cut off the top of Billy's head, we would surely find a bird's nest with eggs.' This early interest grew stronger on my journey towards adolescence, and I latched limpet-like onto anyone with a similar enthusiasm. Luckily, my dad, both grandfathers and many local characters acted as foils to help me along. I already had Jimmy the Ragman as a tutor and mentor – a man I envied for his knowledge of bird and beast – then, good fortune smiled on me once more, and I was introduced to Raffie Gibson.

For well over a year, I travelled into the countryside under the guidance of old Jimmy, during which time I conscientiously listened to the old tinker's lectures on Romany remedies and recipes, trapping animals, fish and birds. Our feathered catches consisted mainly of linnets and redpolls, with goldfinches making up the third finch species regularly taken. My apprenticeship also involved spending many happy hours with Jimmy in the birdshed, assisting in the management of his avian stock.

On a day when I should have been sitting in a stuffy classroom, I was temporarily employed cleaning out birdcages and working out potential permutations for the forthcoming breeding season.

'Did you make these, Jimmy?' I asked, holding a small wire cage in my hand.

'No, lad, I've no patience for that sort of thing. God blessed me with tools for the countryside, not those for factory or garage. Most of them were made by a good friend of mine, Raffie Gibson from Stakeford†. He also makes my trap cages.'

'Does he keep birds?' I questioned, with a frown across my forehead.

'Oh! Yes! He's one hell of a birdman, and a great catcher. I'm going over to his place tomorrow. Do you want to come?'

'Wow! I'd love to. What time?'

'Be here for half past nine. There's a bus at 10 o' clock.'

With such excitement flowing through my veins, the evening progressed on a much slower course. Sleep had to be fought for, but the next morning did eventually come, bringing with it a flurry of snow that left the landscape partially shrouded in a cloak of ermine. As we travelled the short bus ride, Jimmy commented on how we might get out trapping with the weather being as it was. Bad weather is always a great asset to the bird-trapper.

We got off the bus and walked the rest of the journey through a residential estate. The houses were typical of the area, similar to my parents', sturdily built at the beginning of the 20th century, made to endure the test of time. Small gardens lay at the front of the buildings, and much larger spacious grounds to the rear. At an opening,

---

† between Bedlington and Ashington

we turned into a yard dividing two houses. Jimmy approached the green door of the house on the left and gave the shiny, black knocker several hard raps. Continuous drops of water fell from the guttering high above us – the snow had stopped a while ago and was melting as the smiling sun's rays shone through the breaks in the heavy clouds.

The door opened with a crack, as though it had been recently painted. In the entrance stood the small, stout figure of an unshaven man, wearing large, horn-rimmed glasses and a flat cap. He wore a chequered shirt, and the braces that should have been keeping up his heavy-looking, faded, green, corduroy trousers dangled limply around his legs. In a low, gravelly voice, he said,

'Oh! It's you, Jimmy. I nearly shit myself. You knock like the bloody rent man. Hold on a minute, and I'll just get my keys,' and he disappeared back inside the house, closing the door behind him to keep out the bitingly cold air. He returned and came out, slamming the door behind him. He brushed past us, as he sauntered up the yard towards the back garden. He was bow-legged, and this made him rock from side to side as he walked. Without turning around, he murmured,

'Who's the youngin?'

'This is Billy Doherty. I've fetched him to see your birds,' answered Jimmy.

Birdmen from this era rarely possessed a suspicion of visitors or, if they did, they disguised it as well as pewit's eggs on a tilled field. It seemed as though they relished sharing experiences or having the opportunity to show off their birds to others. On this maiden visit, however, I found myself a little frightened of Raffie for some reason.

Once securely in the shed, our host finally acknowledged that I existed.

'Grab a pew, lad,' he said in his deep voice, as I glanced inquisitively around the shed. Ceremoniously, I dusted chaff from the long seat and sat down with my hands tucked submissively under my thighs. Looking towards the cages, I immediately noticed differences to those in Jimmy's shed: these were much more generously proportioned, more like small flight units. Below these cages, flights went the length of the birdroom. They were about a yard high from the floor, and wooden slides divided them into separate sections. These slides looked as though they could all be pulled out to make a really long, single flight, if required.

Fighting for a place on almost every spare piece of wall hung small wire cages, reminiscent of those housing goldfinches and linnets at Jimmy's place. These cages were expertly made, some square in shape, others with rounded tops. Each fine wire had been measured and cut with great precision, then soldered smoothly. The bases were constructed of wood and a small drawer fitted in with a cabinetmaker's exactness to contain seed for any feathered inmate. Like Henry Ford's early vehicles, every cage was painted black.

Raffie broke the shallow silence.

'Been out lately, Jimmy?'

'Aye, Raff, me and the lad here have been getting some bits and pieces, mostly linnets.' I believe Raffie was to some extent impressed with the idea that I was an apprentice bird-trapper, but I felt uneasy as I caught him staring at me.

'Doherty is it? What's your old man's name?'

I removed my gaze bashfully from the cages.

'It's John.'

Raffie raised his cap, as he put his fingers through his hair and slowly scratched his head.

'Did he work at the old Bedlington 'A' Pit?'

'Yes, that's him.'

'Your dad is a hard hitter. Are you a hard hitter?' I looked away sheepishly from the hypnotising clench of his questioning stare.

'I don't know—' Jimmy butted in.

'You're frightening the lad, Raff. He'll tell John on you, mind.' The avenue that the conversation was taking us down prompted me to raise my head and stick out my chest.

'I'm not frightened, Jimmy.' Raffie smiled – I took this as implying that I had been accepted.

'Just joking, lad, just joking, but your dad is a hard hitter.'

Raffie gestured with his pointing finger.

'Go on, then, I know you're dying to have a good look around.'

I had only just begun to feast my eyes on the first cages, when I heard the noise of running water. I turned to see Raffie in the corner of the shed with his back to us; I saw his arm shake a number of times and heard the sound of a zip being pulled up. He strolled over with an old sauce-pan in his hand, opened the door and threw the contents out onto the garden.

'That's better! I needed that.' His voice suggested he was a very relieved man indeed. Now, I was pretty well bursting myself, but there was no way I was going to use that pan as a piss-pot in front of those two. My distracted attention returned to the birdcages, and the unconcerned Raffie took a seat next to Jimmy.

Compared to Jimmy's shed, there were more finches here, but nowhere near as many canaries. The overall quality of the birds, however, was just as good as those at Bedlington. Raffie had a lot of goldfinches and, in the lower flights, quite a few female bullfinches flew back and forth, their white rumps noticeable even in the poor light of these lower compartments. He also possessed a large number of siskins. Pictures of these diminutive finches stuck in my head from bird books, but this was my first opportunity to study them in the feather, so to speak.

I turned to Raffie and Jimmy.

'They're gorgeous. Can you get them around here?' Raffie leaned over slightly in an attempt to see around me.

'Oh! Siskins? Aye, lad, they pay us a visit in the winter, then nick off again at breeding time.' I gazed at them again.

'Are they easy to catch?' Both men answered in harmony,

'Piece of cake!'

Raffie stood up and trundled past me like an old boar badger snorting through a tight gap in a hawthorn hedge, knocking down everything in its wake. Taking a large glass sweet-jar from a shelf, he unscrewed its flat lid and took out a handful of black, shiny niger-seed.

'Watch this,' he said, and he put his seed-filled hand into the cage containing some recently-caught siskins. Within seconds, one of the females landed on his out-stretched palm, pecking furiously at the niger, while cautiously surveying the three pairs of wide, friendly eyes studying her. After a few more moments, two others alighted and fought for places at the dinner table. With his hand still inside the cage, Raffie turned and smiled.

'What do you think of that, then?' What could I say about such a spectacle? Chortling, I glanced at Raffie, turned to Jimmy, then back to Raffie.

'Can I have a go?'

Never will I forget the feel of those tiny feet on the skin of my hand, nor the pin-like probing of the siskin's darting beak. To have a wild bird sit fearlessly that way on your hand was like a win on the pools to a bird-lover like me. This episode is one of many saved in a special place in my mind, an incident that will never be forgotten and that still brings a smile to my face when I sit alone, pondering events from bygone days.

I removed my hand slowly through the narrow door of the cage, the bold siskin waiting till the very last moment before departing, pinching a few last grains of seed before she left a hand that would never have harmed her.

'How did you catch these ones?' I asked. Raffie turned to Jimmy.

'He's coming out of his shell now, isn't he?' he said, referring to the number of questions I was now throwing at him. Jimmy smiled.

'Oh! He's always like that. Wants to know the far end of a fart and which way the stink blows.'

'I caught them with a fishing-rod.'

'Fishing-rod?' I exclaimed. Raffie got up from his seat and walked to a corner of the shed.

'I thought that might get you wondering,' he said, as he took out a fishing-rod bag that had been stuffed down the side of the cages.

Raffie's stumpy, slightly arthritic fingers fumbled as they undid the strap at the top of the long, green canvas bag. He removed, not the usual two, but four lengths of rod, specially adapted so they could all be joined to one another, making overall lengths of either 12, 18 or 24 feet. He wiped dust and grime from the tubular, brass ends, before adding a lubrication of spit and joining them together. Expertly, he demonstrated how a couple of wand sticks are fixed to the end, and how the rod is shoved up into the trees where the siskins are feeding.

'The wands are eased gently towards the bird and, dabbed on its back – one caught siskin,' he said. I was still trying to fathom this out in my mind's eye, and when the word 'wand' was mentioned, I immediately looked in Jimmy's direction, who just shrugged his shoulders and shook his head.

'D–, d–, do they just sit there?'

'They can do, but only in the winter. You've seen what they are like in cages. These birds are naturally tame and, when it's really bad weather, any defences they do possess are let down even further.'

Raffie began to re-bag the rods.

'It's too late now, but if you fancy we can have a look out tomorrow morning for some siskins down by the River Wansbeck.' Jimmy looked towards me.

'I can't go, but you should have a look out. But remember, there are no buses early on a Sunday morning.' My mind was immediately made up.

'Yes, I will go. I'll be here – what time?'

Raffie rubbed his bristly chin.

'I usually leave here early – siskins fly up the river when it's still dark in the morning – but I'll give you time to get here. We will have to be down there for no later than eight o'clock.'

'I will be here for seven, then,' I said, cockily.

No buses; my dad didn't have a car – it looked like I would be biking to Raffie's. If the weather was as bad as it was this morning, I might even be walking the six miles or so.

CHAPTER 6

A FISHER OF BIRDS

The morning was still shackled in darkness when I awoke but, peering through the bedroom window, I could see soft whiteness sparkling as clouds swallowed up the last of the moon's silvery brightness. No snow had fallen overnight, but Jack Frost's icy touch ensured that any remaining scattered patches of white from the day before would lodge with us a little while longer.

Brushing my teeth, I could hear our resident thrush as he sang in the dimness, awoken by dreams perhaps of a future mud-lined home, where, bursting from its cosiness, five wide gapes would demand to be fed.

A sheepish reconnaissance mission outside found paths and roads both treacherous and slippery, but I decided unreservedly to chance a pushbike ride to Raffie's. Gingerly, I set off, with darkness lifting at a snail's pace and with some early birds and beasts beginning to rise from the depths of their burrows and shadowy retreats, rejuvenated by unruffled sleep.

I pedalled past a field of stubble where a group of rooks was already gathering to breakfast, while others appeared from invisible holes in the sky and glided down in the semi-darkness to join their noisy comrades at the buffet table. The sound of the bike's tyres on the crisp, frozen trail crunched above the dawn chorus, and the spectre-like figure of a tawny owl slid silently across my path, its big, wide eyes searching for the twitch of a mouse, vole or shrew. Taking a short-cut up an old farm track that brushed past Simms Wood, I could make out the spider-like branches of trees stretching towards the purple sky. I drove my trusty steed of iron through ice-skinned puddles that cracked like glass under my weight and, although the trail seemed long and winding, I eventually arrived at the bottom of Raffie's lane.

I scurried like a weasel along the street, uncertain whether or not I would be in time. Raffie was just stepping out of the front door as I reached his house.

'You've timed that well, lad. I was just going to get some gear from the shed before I left.'

Now, I was quite educated to old Jimmy's ways, knowing that he would still be there, if I were late. It was apparent there was to be no such luxury with Raffie. If I hadn't made it in time, he would have gone without me.

I followed him to the shed, parking my bike against the grey, concrete coal-bunker. While waiting for him, I gazed at the partially snow-covered garden. Tall, nobly green stalks of sprouts stood erect, their frost-kissed produce hanging tightly, clumped together like bunches of green grapes. A robin rummaged among them in search of a morsel of food – this place he saw as his own and would rigorously defend it against all comers.

Raffie emerged from the shed, his Jack Hargreaves attire convincing even me that he was off to land a fish or two.

'Here, catch!' he said, throwing me the fishing-rod. He slammed the hut door, swung a brown, well-packed haversack over his shoulder and we left.

'I'll carry everything, if you want,' I said to him. He took the rod back from my clutches.

'No, it's all right. I can manage.' It seemed like the robin wasn't the only one wanting to hold on to what he had. This was my maiden voyage with Raffie, so I couldn't expect as smooth a sailing as I had with old Jimmy at the helm.

'Do you think we will get anything, Raffie?'

'Should do – the weather's right. Them siskins' defences will be down; they won't know we are there.' During our expedition, I pointed out every bird that came into sight, as I always did, no matter who I was travelling with. Even footprints in the snow were not safe from my Sherlock Holmes-type detective work. Raffie, with a look of utter disbelief on his face, plodded silently along.

We eventually reached the top of a bank, where, below us, the cold waters of the flooded River Wansbeck roared and hissed as they surged eastwards to meet the North Sea. We clambered cautiously down the steep, wild garlic-carpeted, muddy embankment, using rough steps manufactured by the feet of those who had travelled here before us. Finally reaching the bottom, Raffie pointed towards a sheltered field and, situated at the far side, a collection of fir trees and Scots pines.

'That's what we are making for, lad, them trees up there.'

It was now light, and the full extent of Jack Frost's cold but decorative work was evident, as the countryside awoke on all sides. Branches and twigs on every tree and bush wore gloves of furry ice, which shimmered and glistened as sunlight rested upon them. The solid mud track, stencilled with deep equine hoofprints, barely gave way as we tread cautiously along it. Birds everywhere were full of life, panicking in their hunt for a morsel of food that would help them face the cold.

Raffie's arm came up, halting me in my tracks.

'Look, lad,' and he pointed towards a small charm† of goldfinches picking and probing among the plumes of creeping, welted and cotton-thistle, as well as various other wild plants and grasses along the path's edge. We watched these harlequin-coloured finches flitting like butterflies around the feral herbage. Their ivory beaks prodded frenetically and ripped at the cellulose outer layers to obtain any tiny seeds housed within. It seemed as though they sang as they laboured, their twittering tune broken occasionally by a rapid, scolding burst of *tisst, tisst, tisst*, a warning call advising flock friends to keep their distance. After enjoying the scene for a short while, we carried on. I couldn't help thinking that Raffie would be visiting these parts again, before the advent of spring, armed with a goldfinch callbird and trap cage.

Approaching one end of the evergreens, we paused and Raffie began undoing the long bag and peeling the split cane rods out from their sheath.

'Hold them a minute,' he ordered, passing me a trio of rods. The fourth section was gripped firmly between his arm and chest, so that his thick hands, misshapen with toil, were free to remove a tube containing wands from his haversack. He tore a pair of these straight lime-covered sticks from the tight, sticky bundle and secured them to the end of the rod with clear sticky-tape. He presented me with the finished item, his scrunched stare seeking an opinion.

'There now. We're almost ready,' he said, and we strode towards the high, needle-covered trees.

Apprehension flowed through my veins, as we walked forward, gazing upwards in search of movement among the branches. The only birds to be seen in this section of the copse were a pair of departing wood pigeons, whose white-

† flock

64

barred wings gave a round of applause. Finally, we came upon an alder thicket and a small group of foraging siskins.

'There, lad. Do you see them?'

'Aye, Raffie, but will we get close to them? Those bushes aren't very tall are they?'

'We'll be all right. Just take your time and pass me another length of rod.' Raffie took the stick, wiped the brass ferule on the end and joined the two pieces together.

We inched slowly but surely in the direction of the feeding group. Raffie leant over to whisper.

'You bide here. Get a stow box out of the bag and be ready.' I did as I was bidden, at the same time never taking my gaze from him, as he tiptoed the final short distance through the tangled mass of grass and weeds. To my amazement, the siskins did not seem unduly threatened by our intrusion or by the dark figure approaching them so cautiously, and they continued picking at the hard alder mast. I watched as the long rod was lifted gently and directed upwards through the branches. Closer and closer the sticky wands crept towards their victims, like a mantis rocking to and fro before the final strike. A small flick of the wrist and the wands dabbed across the back of a male siskin. Raffie pulled the rod down quickly and evenly so that it lay behind him on the crisp frost-tainted grass, and removed the squawking bird from the tip. I ran over to him and watched as he partially cleaned the bird, removing a number of lime-soiled feathers in the process.

'There now, pop him in the box,' he whispered. That was the first time I saw a bird being caught in this way – something I had never thought possible.

Without a word, Raffie began tracking the slow-moving siskin group. I followed, out of harm's way, taking a nervous step whenever I had the chance, stealing glimpses of the new acquisition in the carrying box as I inched along. As the rod went aloft once again, I stood motionless, like a heron in a pond of tadpoles. Raffie was surely an expert at this method of catching. His methodical aim was consistently true, like a darts champion singling out a match-winning double top. Again went the flick of the rod, a gentle, whippy strike at another bird. I advanced quickly as the siskin was being gently removed.

'Another cockbird?' I asked.

'Yes,' Raffie replied. He passed the bird to me. 'That's an advantage when catching them this way – you can pick and choose.' It looked very much as though male siskins were the order of the day.

A dozen or so more were taken on that frosty morning, before Raffie asked a question that sent my pulse racing and filled my empty stomach with large cabbage whites.

'Do you want a go?' I felt as vulnerable as a Christian about to face a lion. Part of me was scared; another part of me yelled, Yes! Go on, have a go! The latter was to be the victor on this occasion and received the Emperor's thumbs up. Laying the bag containing our spoils gently on the ground, I walked towards Raffie and, looking through the glasses into the deep pools of his watery eyes, took the rod from his chunky hand.

'Just take your time, lad. There's no hurry. Just take your time.' His words may have been aimed at settling my nerves, but they didn't stop my hands shaking as though I had a hangover from a night on brown ale.

It was my turn to approach the alder thicket where the siskins fed. It felt like I was standing on the centre spot at St James' Park, with all the Newcastle United stands glaring

down at me, so alone and in the open. I sought to turn and see where my teacher was, but I knew what was to be done – it was eggs or chickens now. With a bottomless intake of breath, I began to investigate the branches in front of me. Raffie's words of encouragement echoed through my mind, Just take your time. Don't hurry.

Amid the tangled branches, a separate trio of siskins danced a salsa between twigs, one male and two females. This was my chance. The rod that looked so light and whippy in the hands of my mentor felt like a boat's oar as I began to raise it. Like Raffie, I was going for the cockbird. I shoved the tip of the rod gently towards the olive-green bird, the bright yellow wing flights flashing as it flicked for balance. My nervousness was being transmitted up the full length of the shaft. I clamped both hands on it in an attempt to stop the bloody thing from shaking so much. The bird I was after actually turned and was watching the approaching wands but, astonishingly, made only half-hearted attempts to avoid them. Gradually, I manoeuvred the tip of the rod into a position to strike.

'Slowly now. Take your time, Billy,' I whispered to myself.

I literally just laid the wands onto the back of the bird. What a feeling! What a rush! The nervousness that had flowed through my veins a moment ago left without a trace and I brought the bird down out of the tree.

Raffie came over immediately and began to help me to remove the bird.

'Well done, young Doherty. You look as happy as a pig in shit. How does it feel?'

'Blooming great, Raffie,' my voice trembled. 'Can I have another go?'

'Easy now. Don't get carried away. If you get too excited or eager, you will make mistakes. You can go for another, then we will have to get back – it's getting on. Try for one of those hens, if they are still there.'

As soon as a few feathers were removed from the sticky wand sticks, I was off towards the thicket, fishing-rod in one hand, wiping the gummy fingers of my other down the leg of my trousers. The hen siskins that had accompanied the male had been somewhat startled by the goings on, but they had travelled only as far as the next bush. A combination of the birds' jumpiness and a need to look for food was quickly rebuilding their natural wariness, so this second crack would be a stiffer test for me.

My first attempt at securing one of this pair saw them going to the far side of the bush. I circumnavigated to get a better shot at them, but they moved back towards their original position. A game of cat and mouse ensued. I could see through the branches that Raffie was beckoning me to return, shaking his head as though to say it was no good chasing them that way. Still hyped up by my maiden success, I thought to myself, One final go.

The pair must have become weary of the game too, but settled momentarily. Taking full advantage, I aimed the tip of the rod towards them, at the last moment singling one of them out. Quickness of wrist, which was absent when I took my first bird, played a big part this time. The gluey sticks touched the back and one open wing just as the bird decided it was time to leave. This was another one in the bag for Billy.

Walking in the direction of Raffie, I said,

'I thought I wasn't going to get that one.'

'Aye, you did well. I would have given up long ago.' The

stow box in Raffie's hand was all set to take the bird, which was already separated from the wands. I slid it in through the partly-opened lid, and we both peered in through the wire front.

'That's it for today my fine, fishing friend. Time to make tracks.'

This was my first trip out with Raffie catching birds. We eventually became great friends, and he shared his time with me on many other occasions. Raffie taught me a great deal during my time with him, a period I cannot measure in years. As Homer once said, 'A year in the lifetime of a sheep is only equal to a moment in the life of a tiger.'

Raffie was a very much better bird-breeder than old Jimmy, and he introduced me to many of his tricks of the trade, when attempting to 'go agin nature' and produce wonderful finch-cross-canary mules. He was also the first man to show and educate me in the ways and benefits of soaking seed, as a conditioner as well as a helpful rearing foodstuff.

Whenever I required a trap cage or an all-wire cage constructed to the highest quality, I called in at Raffie's place, and I experienced the depths of despair when I was told of his death many years later. This one is for you, Raffie my old friend, the birdman who helped me grow up and taught me how to be a 'fisher of birds'.

CHAPTER 7

BILL OGLE

O f all the birdmen known to me during my lifetime, none deserve the title of bird-catcher more than old Bill Ogle. This man's knowledge and understanding of small passerines was prodigious, and his skill in taking all species of finches using every available trapping method was the envy of his contemporaries.

Bill lived in a semi-detached council house. The spacious rear garden was positioned so that it pointed in the direction of my old friend Raffie's home. In fact, Raffie's birdshed could be seen from the window of Bill's big, black lean-to. This housing estate had begotten at least half a dozen bird-trappers – something in the water I do believe. Finches passing overhead in undulating flight ran a gauntlet of callbirds and lures to reach feeding grounds bordering Simms Wood. The gardens of these birdmen were probably among their most productive catchment areas over a season. Whereas illicit ventures into the local, finch-abundant countryside would be a regular occurrence for trappers in the hostile winter months, trap cages or flap nets were permanent features on their private grounds. Many birds, such as goldfinches, linnets and redpolls, were captured while eager eyes observed the happenings through peepholes bored into the sides of birdsheds or from the windows of cosy living-rooms.

The name Ogle was well known in bird circles in this part of Mid Northumberland, and I heard it mentioned many times by various people. In those days in the exhibition world, it was not necessarily a matter of who could breed the top British bird exhibit. In the majority of cases, it was more a question of who could catch the best. Many of the finches that won the highest accolades at the local Northumbrian cagebird-society shows emanated from Bill Ogle and his big flight in the sky.

My initial visit to the Ogle residence saw me standing solitary at the side door, knocking nervously as I waited for a man I didn't know, hadn't seen and had only heard of. Eventually, the door opened. It's funny at times, when you constantly hear of someone of stature in a pastime or hobby you are interested in, how you conjure up a mental picture of the person. I was expecting a hybrid between John L. Sullivan and Henry Cooper, but standing in front of me was a Charles Hawtrey look-alike from the Carry On films, wearing black National Health spectacles and a cowboy hat. He wore a smart, black suit, with a gold, Albert-chain draped from one side to the other of a neatly-fastened, matching waistcoat. A crimson, Gypsy-style cravat adorned his neck. There seemed to be an epidemic of wearing cravats – a must in the attire of serious bird-trappers, it seemed.

For a split second, I was lost for words. I could hardly speak, as though my teeth were glued by a well-sucked toffee, and he just stood there looking at this small, scruffy person and trying to figure out whether it was the time of year for carol singers or a penny for the guy.

'Aye, lad, can I help you?' The ice was broken, and my speech was quickly restored.

'My name's Billy Doherty and I've heard you keep birds. Raffie from over the back said I should visit you.' And I pointed in the general direction of Raffie's abode. Now, I

could hardly have been taken for an RSPCA man or a plain-clothes policeman out to arrest him for his illicit leisure pursuits, but I wasn't sure whether he would appreciate such a poor, unsolicited introduction.

The old man stepped out of the house.

'Raffie has mentioned your name and told me you might be coming over sometime.' He called into the house before closing the door,

'Marion, I'm away to the birdshed.' He seemed in no way concerned about allowing me a personal viewing of his birds. He walked up the backyard silently in front of me, his gait slow and methodical as he sauntered with pomp, style and grace. I followed like a humble servant. His grabbing hand searched the deep, jingling pockets of his trousers for the shed keys and, at the same time, he murmured,

'I haven't got much in for you to see at the moment.'

We weaved around bins, steel buckets and half a load of coal spewing from a sloping-topped coal-bunker, then along a narrow path of cracked and chipped flagstones laid unevenly around the edge of his shed. The front of the hut was completely adorned with small-panelled, metal window-frames, cast-offs from when the houses were renovated a few years before.

Nothing went to waste in those days. Sheds were constructed from thrown-out spars and inch-thick wooden floorboards; leek trenches were lined with panelled, hardwood doors and greenhouses were assembled using strong, metal windowframes. None of these were aesthetically pleasing, but the unmaterialistic owners were proud of them nevertheless.

On entering the sanctuary of the shed, I was very much taken aback by its interior design and layout. There were only a token number of canary-sized breeding cages, with a few of the customary, larger flights in the darker spaces between these and the shed floor. A wooden ledge held many wire cages, with flighty goldfinches, obviously freshly caught, jumping to and fro inside them. My main surprise was that the shed looked really big from the outside, but so diminutive and compact inside.

'These are my cages and flights, and I have a large aviary behind there,' and he pointed towards the far side of the shed. He walked to the wall and peered through a small, glass-fronted hole purposely cut into the wood.

'Go on, get yourself a look,' and he stood back to allow me a view. I examined the contents of the secret enclosure. It was a vast area that possessed a rich soil floor, a base where moss and discarded, soaked seeds would always do better than marigolds and daffodils. Branches of conifer and broom decorated the wooden walls, some fresh in olive-green, others tired, dry and russet-brown. Windows half-covered the south-facing side of the aviary, allowing the sun's warmth to illuminate the whole space, giving a fresh look and feel to it – an ideal, natural-looking environment for breeding birds in, I thought.

'There's a goldfinch cock and a bullie hen in there somewhere,' he told me, as he gently shoved my face from the viewing opening with his head. 'Ah! There they are – over to the right. Can you see them?' he pointed, allowing me space once again to survey the enclosure.

'Yes, I see them.' Both birds sat compatibly on the same sprig of evergreen, which gently bounced under their weight.

'They're well paired up them two; they've been together all though the winter,' he said.

'Have you ever bred them before?'

'No, son. I've tried every year for a long time now; had eggs from other pairs – fertile eggs, but no chicks.' I slowly left the let-hole and sat down on the seat under the window.

'It must have taken some nerve to come and see me alone and unannounced like that,' he said. Although he was correct in his statement, I disguised the fact like a lark's nest in grass and answered,

'No, not really.'

'Well now, lad. This is all I have in,' and he pointed to the flighty goldfinches, and behind them, quite unconcerned in the breeding cages, a number of wee gems†. In the confinement of the lower flights, a number of female bullfinches tried to hide among the conifer branches packed in at either end, their stooping heads watching my every movement as I attempted to get a better view of them.

Even at such a tender age, I was capable of sussing out Bill Ogle. His shed was set up for a quick turnover of birds, caught in one day and moved on the next. He was predominently a trapper, and the various trap cages and nets that fought for room on the walls advertised this fact well. Fatalities were never thrown onto the compost heap, but expertly opened up via their breasts and their flesh removed. The remaining feathered carcase would be doused in borax, filled with cotton wool and stitched up. A fine, springy type of wire was inserted into the body, the wings were spread and secured, and the whole thing left to dry. These unrefined examples of taxidermy would never last the 100 or so years' expected of a professionally-mounted subject, but they did fulfil the short-term function of being fitted to the tops of

†border canaries

ripe thistle heads, to help lure others of their kind down to the tacky wand sticks.

Bill did enjoy doing a certain amount of breeding, not as much as Jimmy, and certainly not nearly as much as Raffie. Everything would be for sale in this avian hypermarket, although at the time I was pretty low down in the pecking order of people wanting birds from him – but that would change.

Bill's hearing was poor and deteriorated at an alarming rate during the time I was under his wing. I would go trapping with him as his ears, an early warning system for approaching birds, and even to tell him whether the Judas callbird was doing its job efficiently. Many times, when hiding beneath dew-soaked bushes or behind closely-planted trees in dense, bullfinch-infested woods, I would say, 'Bill, Bill! Quiet! They're coming.' He would immediately discontinue his conversation, talk magnified by an inability to hear his own voice properly; he would then strain to hear the soft piping calls of the rose-breasted bullies as they approached unseen. In return for my assistance, he taught me much of what I know and gave me first pick of any newly-caught birds. More importantly, he convinced me that I should spend more time in the classroom and restrict my clandestine meetings with mother nature to weekends and holidays.

While at school, there weren't many lessons I relished. I was a good footballer and athlete, representing both junior and senior school football teams during the same term. On sports day, just for the sheer hell of it, I entered every discipline, sometimes having to start one event just as another ended. Bill's good advice was heeded, but I remained determined to visit all my old bird-keeping mates, although maybe not as often as I had in the past.

Bill's shed was a Shangri-la of interests, where he taught me many incredible trapping skills and, also, what birds do and why they do it. He showed me how to determine accurately the gender of certain species that were usually difficult to sex, and how to age a bird by the shape of the tips of its wing and tail flights, the condition and wear of its feathers and its moult cycle. My keen interest in wildlife and in learning the ways of the fields did sometimes have an effect on my time at school, but not always for the worst. Like when the care-taker once reported me to the headmaster for setting a trap cage to catch goldfinches among some bushes of dog-rose, box and privet in the school grounds. Luckily the headmaster didn't have the same enthusiasm for such rules and regula-tions as the informant, who belonged to that awkward class of park-keepers, cinema attendants and social-club doormen. The tweed-jacketed tutor just shook his head in utter disbelief and took great pleasure in learning more about the technical workings of the trap cage, once the supergrass was dismissed from the study to the words of, 'Thank you for bringing this to my attention, Mr Jackson.'

On another occasion, I sold a rather nice, recently caught-in goldfinch cock at the pricey sum of five shillings to the English teacher, Mrs Hagen, whose husband, a retired teacher, was a keen bird-keeper and breeder of canaries and required a male finch from which to breed mules.

Bill Ogle was also the man who let me into the trapper's trade secret of making bird-lime, when others, rightly or wrongly, attempted to keep it from me. This is the glue-like substance that covered the wand sticks, adhering to its feath-ered victims in such a way that they could neither move nor escape. Traditionally, bird-lime was made from the bark of the holly bush. It was collected during the warm summer months and underwent a number of lengthy, bizarre procedures before being ready for use. It possessed incredible tackiness, and would neither freeze in the winter, nor run in warmer temperatures. Other nostrums and potions for making bird-lime ranged from those which were too sticky, to those which were not tacky enough, while others went solid in the cold, rendering them quite useless. At one time, before any legislation had been implemented to outlaw taking birds from the wild, a pot of resin-based bird-lime could be purchased from almost any chemist for tuppence.

One recipe I was told of consisted of melting crêpe, a rubber like substance used many years ago for the soles of shoes. To this, linseed oil was added to prevent it returning to a solid state. Still at a tender age – in my pre-Bill Ogle days – this sounded quite a feasible idea; furthermore, I was determined to have my own supply and decided to put my limited chemistry prowess to the test and give it a go.

First I obtained my supplies. A short journey ensued to Rockets Shoe Repairs, where I was greeted by a percussion solo of machinery and a man in a soiled brown coat.

'A piece of crêpe sole, please.'

'What size?' he asked, in a tone that suggested he was trying to catch me out.

'Oh! About so big,' and I illustrated with my fingers roughly the dimensions of a postcard. He disappeared through a door and returned, slapping a piece of white crêpe on the polished-wood counter.

'Four pence,' he demanded. I dug deep into my pocket, paid the man and left. All the way home, I bent, played with and stared at my purchase. Who would think that such an article as a piece of rubber could hold such fascination?

From our rubbish bin, I took an empty baked-bean can,

washed it out and removed the paper label that was already beginning to peel. My makeshift Bunsen burner was two full and two half house-bricks, positioned so that rolled-up pieces of paper, cardboard, sticks and small lumps of coal could be stacked and set alight. The canister containing the crêpe sole sat leaning among the licking flames, and soon the contents began to bubble and melt. Linseed oil was added, and a thick, brown smoke billowed upwards from the chimney-like tin. My inquisitiveness got the better of me, and I positioned my face among the rising smog to find out what it smelt like. Such a distinctive blend of chemicals not only produced gases that were possibly toxic, but also unstable and volatile. At that precise moment, the smoke ignited, and my head was engulfed in a ball of fire. The stench of burnt hair filled the air. My fingers searched around my forehead for eyebrows and a fringe that had dissolved like a genie disappearing back into its lamp. I ran into the house and doused my face with copious amounts of water. Looking into the mirror to ascertain the extent of the damage, the vermilion blaze of a goldfinch was the first thought that entered my head. My cheeks were as red as a traffic light at stop, my forehead even redder. My lucky escape was due more to good fortune rather than good management, and a black mark was issued to the other idiot who had suggested the formula in the first place. At this point, I could almost hear Jimmy the Ragman's warning about wands and bird-lime ringing in my blistered ears: I told you so.

Now, all those years ago, everyone possessed a bird's-egg collection, and I responded to the thrill and excitement of searching for the nests of wildlings and their jewels just like everyone else, and so did old Bill. I saw myself as a dab-hand bird-nester and could usually find the home of any bird fairly easily, but Bill allowed me into his secret of how to hear the location of a bird's home and how to find one without hardly even touching a branch.

Together, we would walk through fields or along quiet country lanes listening for male finches singing. A goldfinch on a high perch or telephone wire, a linnet swaying on a sprig of gorse or a greenfinch on the top, broad-leaved branch of an elderberry bush. These were the tell-tale signs Bill would hunt for. He told me,

'When a female bird sits on her clutch, she has to be there alone for nearly two weeks. The only pacifications for her are the fact that she can hear her mate singing or his occasional visit with a morsel of food.' He used to say that if you found a cockbird serenading his true love, the matrimonial home wouldn't be very far away. It was truly amazing how this premise was proved correct time and time again.

When we first embarked on our joint bird-nesting forays in search of linnets, Bill also corrected my pulling each prickly branch of gorse to one side, or crouching on all fours to look up into the bush.

'Let the stick do the work,' he ordered and would pace around the spiky fortresses, beating the golden-flowered boughs with the seasoned length of hazel he always carried with him on such expeditions. On hearing the fluttering of wings disturbed by Bill's noisy invasion, the area was explored until the nest was found.

Bill's motivation for bird-nesting wasn't the same as mine. My fascination lay in the excitement of finding a nest, taking an egg, carefully making a small hole in either end with a pin and blowing out the contents. The hollow egg was added to my collection of countless others from differing parentages in sawdust-filled shoe boxes. Any nests belonging to linnets or goldfinches found by Bill were robbed, nest and all; the precious eggs were carefully transferred to sitting canaries, surrogate parents employed to raise the chicks as though they were their own. This gave Bill the opportunity to fit the correct-sized closed rings which would help command a higher price if for sale, and to have in his possession fledglings that never experienced the wild, so that they would be easier to manage and hopefully breed from, either crossbred or true.

I remember one fine, mid-summer day finding the shallow untidy nest of a bullfinch, constructed so sparsely with sticks and dried-out bramble stalks that daylight could be seen through it. This nest possessed six pale, blue eggs, with a small number of markings at the larger, rounded end. On this occasion, I never removed my usual reward, as a nest with a full clutch meant these eggs could have already started to turn and the forming chick would be nigh impossible to blow out.

I visited Bill the next day, eager to tell him of my ornithological find.

'Can't use them. Nothing rears young bullies – it's a waste of time,' he said, almost apologetically. The old man watched as the expression on my face changed instantly from an excited smile to glum disappointment.

'I might have an idea though.'

I led Bill to the location of the hidden nest and he carefully parted the branches. The black-capped, chocolate-coloured female sat tight as his hand approached her. I could see the look of fear deep in her lustrous eyes as Bill's brown fingers rested on the rim of her nest. With less than an inch to spare, she exploded from her clocking†, piping angrily as she disappeared into the depths of the scrub. Bill removed one of the

†clucking, incubating

83

warm eggs and held it up between his forefinger and thumb towards the bright, indigo sky.

'These are almost ready for hatching, Billy lad. That's all I wanted to know.'

During the ensuing days, Bill kept vigil over the bullie's nest like an expectant father. The chicks eventually hatched and, at around six days of age, each was fitted with a brown, D-sized, closed ring, obtained through the exchange of a linnet cock with another local birdman. In just under another two weeks, the nest was completely covered by a domed piece of fine-meshed wire-netting. This stopped the youngsters, who were now pretty well feathered up, from leaving the nest that had almost served its purpose. The loyal parent birds, however, could still find the wide hungry gapes in order to feed them. On his visits, Bill also kept the babies topped up with food through the mesh, getting them used to his intervention, and he monitored their rate of growth until experience told him the time was right to remove the potential fledglings, which, as luck would have it, coincided with my being off school.

We took the nest of chicks to Bill's. A baby food was prepared consisting of hardboiled egg yolk, suet and Thomas' condition food; this was chewed up into a moist consistency in our cement mixer-like mouths. How I delighted in feeding those little birds, filling their purple mouths from the tip of a match stick as their wings fluttered with approval. All day Saturday and all day Sunday, I sat in the confines of Bill's shed handling and feeding the young bullfinches, which, when not on my fingers, were already picking at the soaked seed and chickweed on the floor of their cage – although more through inquisitiveness than through knowing what they were doing.

After this exhilarating and most stimulating weekend,

it was seven long days before I could return to Bill's. When I did, I found all six chicks were up off the floor, jumping about and playing, and I'm sure they were as pleased to see me as I was them.

'Looking well, aren't they?' Bill proudly asked.

'Great,' I replied, smiling and gazing long and hard at the vivacious youngsters. Bill filled a shallow dish with water and put it into the cage. One by one the youngsters sat unsteadily on the edge, examining the container's contents. Then after a short game of dare, there was a communal bath, which left them saturated and bedraggled.

All those bullies made it to adulthood – testimony to old Bill's expertise and, of course, with a little assistance from yours truly. The true parents of the bullie chicks were forgotten about during this halcyon period but, with it being the time of the year it was, they had probably produced another clutch before the end of the season, with many more beautiful offspring to adorn our woods, parks and quiet country lanes.

Bill's passion for taking from the wild and rearing finch chicks was demonstrated again a year later, when a goldfinch unwittingly built a home in a broad-leaved lilac bush that decorated a neighbour's garden, a little too close to escape Bill's keen, magpie-like eye. The tiny, beautifully-constructed nest on the uppermost tip of the highest branch, however, was found late, and the chicks were too big to ring. At a little over two weeks old, the youngsters were taken carefully. I say carefully, as goldfinch chicks, along with those of linnets, are notorious for exploding from their nests at this age, whenever there is the slightest hint of danger. No hand-rearing for me on this occasion, as Bill's game plan was completely different from the young bullfinch episode.

Through the day, all five fluttering goldfinch chicks were temporarily housed in a wooden No 2 British bird show cage. This was placed on the side of Bill's shed, facing the bush where they were born. The whimpering cries of the young goldfinches wanting to be fed immediately attracted the attentions of the parent birds. Every day, the loyal adults visited the cage, alighting on the wire front and topping up each demanding mouth. The floor of the cage was covered with seeded chickweed to invite the youngsters to pick. Gradually, over a number of days soaked seed was also placed on the cage floor and, by this time, the fledglings' curiosity directed itself towards the food offered and they began to crack open the softened kernels. Nature designed young birds to learn and equip themselves very quickly in order to survive in a potentially hostile world. After a week in Bill's possession, the chicks' tails had lengthened, they were stronger, they yelped and called less and could virtually fend for themselves. The parent goldfinches still visited but, noticeably, not as frequently.

On my customary early Saturday morning call, Bill was just about to transfer the group into the cage. However, on this occasion, it wasn't the show cage that would be their home for the day. All the chicks were assembled in the bottom section of a double drop-in trap cage.

'Are you going to catch the old 'ns?' I asked, disbelievingly.

'Aye, that's the general idea, lad,' and he brushed past me quite emotionlessly with the all-wire device in his hands. This cage was hung on the same nail as usual, and Bill returned, just as the adult birds appeared to visit their chicks, both of them swaying on the top branches of the lilac bush, swishing their tails and calling.

Bill Ogle

It is not an uncommon phenomenon for a particular species of bird to fly on a well-used flight path, or to frequent a certain feeding or drinking place at the same time almost every day. The habitual route was followed by the goldfinches to their brood. The male bird clung to the side of the cage, his tail swishing from side to side as he called his welcome. The hen stood on the top of the cage, looking down at her family through a small amount of strategically-placed chickweed. She too was pleased to see them and proud-tailed with it. We observed as always through holes drilled in the side of the shed. I watched as the female alighted onto the trap's activating platform and saw the bright yellow of her wings flutter as the trap clicked. She was caught. The startled male flew up and landed on a wire that ran past Bill's home.

'One down and one to go,' Bill stated coldly.

'Do you think he'll come back?' I asked.

'Got to – that's his missus and bairns in there. He'll come down.' Just as the old man predicted, the cock goldfinch soon dipped down toward the cage. Through my peep hole, I could see this was a fair example of a goldfinch: his colours were rich and his black wing flashes were conspicuous because they lacked the usual white-button markings†. He strutted around the top of the trap like a bantam cock. He was still a little nervous and flighty, and his wings twitched with every noise or movement. Then he too was lured into the ambush, as the trap shouted, I've got him. This whole affair demonstrated to me how ruthless old Bill was as a trapper. I would have probably settled for the youngsters, and the thought of taking the parents too would never have entered my head.

†a sign of breeding condition

87

A Bird in the Hand

CHAPTER 8

BILLY BULLFINCH

As with most of my elder trapping comrades, Bill Ogle lived a fair distance from my parents' home in Bedlington. Any visits to his abode or jaunts travelling by his side into the fields meant a long walk or a swift ride on my two-wheeled stallion.

It was the eve of Guy Fawkes' Night when a plan was mastered with military precision by Bill and me to visit a dene on the sloping north banks of the River Wansbeck, below the terraced mining houses of Old North Seaton. This coarse wooded area that led down to the lapping water's edge was renowned for its endemic bullfinch population. These birds found fulfilment feeding greedily on the red fruit of hawthorn and rowan, or ground plants such as meadowsweet and dock. Many local trappers frequented the area to reap some of its rich pickings.

Bullfinches at that time were highly prized in bird circles, and were probably third in popularity – behind goldfinches and linnets – among finches sought after for trapping. Although the male of the species is a bold and handsome chap with rose-pink breast, slate-blue back and contrasting clean-cut, ebony hood, it is the hen bird that attracts most of the bird-trapper's attentions. Between the two sexes, it is only the female that has proved her worth as a hybridiser, crossbreeding in captivity with male goldfinches, linnets, greenfinches, redpolls and domesticated canaries. As a species to breed true, they can be a little fickle and unpredictable at times, and fanciers either have the knack of success with them or they don't. They certainly cannot be classed as the novice's ideal bird, although it is surprising how many aviculturalists would keep a pair of bullies in their flights, as a wonderful species to observe, or just in case they did turn out the odd nest of chicks.

November heralds the beginning of winter and, for me, evokes a sense of what is happening in the fields, woods and hedgerows at this time of the year: the angry gales of September and October have blown themselves out; the daylight hours are getting shorter and greyer; wildlife in its many guises is ebbing towards peaceful slumber: a solemn stillness remains and mornings are either damp or patterned with Jack Frost's wanderings. So the early part of my voyage to the pre-determined meeting place with old Bill was guaranteed to be dark and cold, but a sense of warmth was to greet me in the form of an old friend.

As I pushed my bike down the yard towards the street, who should be sauntering towards me without a care in the world but my canine chum, Duke.

'Hello, fella! Has old woman Purdy kicked you out then?' Duke pressed his side against my leg. His silky hair felt as cold as a deserted clutch of eggs as I patted and rubbed him. His mistress was getting well on in years, and her mind wandered as much as her dog; she had probably thought he was asleep under the table when she locked the door the previous evening.

'I'm off on a special mission this morning,' I said to the dog, as he looked up at me with intelligent eyes. 'You can't come this time. Go on now, off you go! Get yerself home,' and I pointed in the direction of Albert Road, where he lived. Mounting my bike, I set off in the opposite direction, but Duke being Duke took no heed of my orders. He could sense the excitement I had attempted to hide from him behind my harsh words and was having none of that go-home lark. I heard the clipping sound of his nails behind me as I rode. I pedalled faster to see him off and hopefully to make him give up his tag-along, but it was no good. I slowed down to a stop.

'You're not going to give in, are you?' I asked him. 'Come on, then, you can come. Don't know how Bill's going to take it.' And I set off again at a rate of knots that Duke could comfortably follow.

In due course, I arrived at the meeting place, where Bill stood silhouetted in the grey light like some detective off the telly, next to a post holding a pointing sign that displayed the words, Public Footpath.

'I see you've brought a friend.'

'Yes, this is Duke. He's all right. He knows the crack. He won't say a word,' I said, apologetically. Bill wasn't at all angry at the dog's intrusion on our jaunt, and he gently stroked Duke's head.

'We're after bullfinches not rabbits,' he said to the dog, and Duke responded with a friendly lick of Bill's hand and his customary nudge into the old man's nether regions. I turned to bury my laughter and went to lay my bike in the first clump of briars adjacent to the path, concealing it with handfuls of dried grass.

Bill lifted the small rucksack from the cold pavement and, rubbing at the dull pain in the crotch of his pants, limped past me.

'Come on, lad. No time to waste,' he wheezed.

For the first time on this soggy morning, Duke and I were walking on soft ground, with decaying leaves forming a slippery, brown carpet beneath us. Daylight was slowly but surely winning its skirmish with the night, a blackbird that had stored away his flutes for the night began to pipe and, in front of us, a raucous alarm rang out in the bushes as a roosting pheasant was disturbed.

I had walked this partly-overgrown lane to the river in the past with old Bill, and earlier with Raffie. Last season, at the turn of the year, I had operated as Bill's ears, listening for flocks of siskins flying up the course of the river in the darkness. I could recall Bill's dancing fingers as they hurriedly set trap cages and adjusted the position of wand sticks, in preparation for the advent of the tiny green invaders from the pine forests, once I had warned him they were on their way.

Although Bill drove us on because of the ensuing daylight, he walked in a quite unruffled manner – but this was Bill: never in a hurry, just so methodical and efficient in his gait. He occasionally stopped to pick some of the tall-stemmed dock that was growing by the path's edge, bundling them up in his hand like a bunch of flowers. Duke dawdled behind and then zipped past us before stopping dead in his tracks, finding an interesting scent that lay buried in the grass. Even in darkness, I felt secure and at home in such a countryside setting where time, for the moment, was forgotten. The soft, welcoming glow of distant farm and cottage lamps replaced those intense illuminations of the town we had left behind us.

The river was close now and, although it didn't have

the roar and hiss of the sea it flows into, you could sense its presence, even though thick bushes and semi-darkness prevented your eyes from seeing its strength and splendour.

'This way,' Bill ushered, and we left the track, stooping into a corridor in the trees. We inched our way through, as inquisitive branches touched our faces and tangled, snatching fingers of bramble and briar tried their best to trip us. Emerging, we found a grass-covered inlet stretching towards the shimmering water, steep gorse-covered banks sloping at our flanks and the bushes we had come through forming a barrier to our rear.

'This will do nicely,' said Bill, as he plonked the bag on the damp ground.

Bill strode to the centre of the clearing. I followed, feeling the quietness, listening to the sounds which enhanced the stillness of this tranquil new world: the water's soft lapping on the shingle tide-line; a secretive rustle of leaves as a shy rabbit bounded between burrows; and, in the distance, a sheep's querulous, trembling bleating.

The old man bent down and jostled with two of the red-seeded dock stems, pushing them into the soft earth, both set at angles to the ground, pointing in opposite directions.

'Bring me the caller from the bag, Billy.' I ran to fetch the bird and, as I was opening the flap, the bullfinch in the cage piped a few notes. Immediately, a response of soft calls came from the bushes around me. Our quarry was already here – the whole area was a roosting place. Bill had surely done his homework for this morning's work.

'Bill, Bill! There's bullies in the bushes,' I whispered

excitedly, as I returned. 'I could here them calling above me, hundreds of them.' – Clearly an exaggeration of the truth born of sheer excitement.

Silently, Bill took the wire drop-in trap from me. I studied him as he placed it between the two dock stalks and then set the trap. He added two sticky wand sticks to each dock. These were placed, one near the base and one close to the top of the plant, and all the wands were positioned pointing back to the ground.

'There now, let's get back to the bushes,' Bill said, as he walked backwards from the trap, checking everything was right. We made for a darker more secluded corner, away from the opening from which we had emerged earlier. As we positioned ourselves among the foliage, I could hear the continuous piping between the callbird and the bullfinches in the trees.

'Can you hear anything?'

'Yes, Bill, they're calling all the time.'

We sat uncomfortably on the wintry earth, with Duke pinned to the ground between us, a position which, from his continuous struggling and twitching, he didn't relish. From all around us, the fanfare of piping bull-finches echoed. The sharp *tic, tic* call of an inquisitive robin joined in as he hopped in front of us among the rotten leaves.

With squinting eyes, I suddenly saw the white rump of a bullfinch bobbing towards the ambush. The bird by-passed the docks and alighted on the edge of the cage and, as though in hurry, dived headlong into the trap.

'Hold the dog,' Bill said, as he arose calmly and, then, glancing all around, he strode one hand in pocket to-wards the trap. Duke and I watched eagerly, as he knelt at the trap before returning with a cock bullfinch in the grip of his hand. He showed me the bird. Its beak was wide open in a threatening manner, exposing its purple lined gullet. I had done enough training in the trapping vocation now to realise that I was expected to have the stow at the ready. Bill popped the bird through the small round door, which I fastened securely.

Still the calling of wild bullfinches in the bushes rained down on us; faint calls became louder as the birds got closer and closer. In a flash, another bullfinch visited the cage and was safely locked in. Again, it was a male; and so were the next two.

'All bloody cocks!' Bill exclaimed. 'We could do with some hens.'

'At least they've all been caught in the trap, Bill.'

'Aye, nice and clean, I suppose,' his voice full of sarcasm.

A short time elapsed before more bullfinches made their way through the bushes, where from every branch, veils of gossamer now hung heavily, speckled with diamond-like droplets of dew that glittered in the growing morning light. This time, a pair dropped towards the trap cage. One bird landed on the ground close to the cage, while the other stood on the side of the open trap, angrily flapping its wings, head cocked to one side, peering down at the callbird. The bullfinch on the ground flitted to climb the inviting, seeded dock stem. It tumbled stiffly as though rigor mortis had suddenly set in to its delicate body, landing with the wand stick fast across its torso and an outstretched wing. Bill lifted as quickly as I had ever seen him move and actually ran towards the cage. The second bullfinch, startled by the old man's

ungainly bounding, flew to safety amid the top swaying branches of a nearby hawthorn.

Bill removed the wand smoothly, got rid of any feathers from the fine stick and replaced it on the dock, then returned smartly, cleaning the contaminated feathering of the bird as he loomed towards Duke and me.

'Hen at last, Billy lad.' He confirmed the bird's gender, showing me her chocolate colouration. Duke's wet nose pushed upwards, his eyes bright and wide, so that he too could have a look. The other bullfinch remained unsteady on its high perch.

'Do you think he will come down, Bill?' I asked, as I locked the door of the stow box.

'Don't think so. Bullies bond strongly during the breeding season, but this trait isn't carried on into the latter part of the year – one of nature's safeguards to curtail breeding too close. That cockbird is a rover: he will move on to another area and another hen, and a new cock bully will take his place.'

Just as Bill forecast, the male bullfinch took one last look towards us, dipped and took off in the direction of the river.

It was fairly light now. How these wintry woods differed from when I visited them in the summer during bird-nesting expeditions with my old companion, Bill, I thought to myself. The bushes and trees may have been the same, only tireder, the grass may have been the same carpet we walked on, just a little worse for wear, but the whole place just felt different – a sense of dampness had replaced the replenishing season's warmth and echoing thrill of vibrant life.

The rate at which we were now collecting bullfinches

began to decrease. However, the law of averages could be seen at work and a number of hens were secured, much to Bill's pleasure.

'We have a canny number there now. We'll give it a little while longer and then pack up – it's getting on,' Bill said, so hesitantly that I knew that he, like me, could have sat in our cosy camp for the rest of the day. A moment or two later and, after a short piping introduction, another hen bullfinch dropped to the cage. This bird seemed more hesitant than any of the others we had caught that morning. She clambered cautiously round the top of the trap, then, at the point when I thought that was that and that she would fly off, she dropped into the cage. Bill took hold of the dog's neck and, surprisingly, offered me the opportunity to collect the spoils.

'Go on! Go and get her.'

I accepted his offer with alacrity. The bird darted and dashed about in the confines of the trap as I approached. Lifting the lid, I slid my hand in, driving her to the corner, where I took her gently in my grasp. Her brown feathering had a purple hue. She was relatively small for a bullfinch hen, but very well coloured, while her feathering was tight and sleek.

After this bird was added to the others, and when the customary stare through the wires of the stow box was done, Bill made his way to the trap to collect the callbird and the wands. Duke, having been starved of adventure for a long while, followed the old man; he sniffed around the cage, before realising it held nothing of interest and made off for the bushes. I sorted out the bags and boxes, before joining Bill.

We were privileged to account for a total of nine bullfinches that morning, five cocks and four hens. As my pay, I was later given a trio of bullfinches, two males and a hen.

When all was packed up, we left for our homeward journey, but not before our last bit of excitement for the day. Duke, who had shown a lot of interest in a certain patch of gorse, put up a squatting rabbit that lay in the bushes' densest shadows. The creature crashed through the thicket with the dog close behind. Then we got our first proper sighting, as the pair burst like a couple of cannon balls from a patch of taller grass. The rabbit broke out onto the only area of open ground, its intention to find sanctuary in the bushes across the way, but this was to be its downfall. Duke was a very fast dog over short distances. He would be hard-pressed to equal a quick-footed hare but, against this less formidable opponent, he was a safe bet. As he closed in, the screams of a rabbit that knew it was beaten rang out. The dog's head dipped, his jaws locking across the back of his prey, his head lifted and, after a swift, spine-breaking crunch, the screams were no more.

'Go on!' Bill cried out. 'That's the best chase of a rabbit I've seen for years. He can turn on a tanner, that un.' Duke carried the rabbit back to me as he always did, even though he didn't have a single retrieving lesson to his credit.

'Well done, Duke, well done,' I praised, at the same time patting and rubbing his black fur, wet with moisture from the bushes.

'Here, Bill, a pie!' and I passed the rabbit over.

Bill's eyes lit up.

'I'll get wor lass to cook this when I get back – get

some onions, mushrooms and black pudding.' I must admit that talk like that made my mouth water. My faithful canine hunting companion might have foraged out another before we got back to my bike, but alas he didn't – there would be other times though.

Bill Ogle's entire life had been geared up for his love of and interest in birds. He wasn't a materialistic man and never sought after wealth or great riches. Bill typified Thoreau's statement that 'A man is rich in proportion to the number of things he can do without.'

Bill and I were great friends for many years. When I was old enough to drive, I regularly took my old mate for his pension, to the doctor's or dropped him off for a pint at his favourite ale-house. After the death of his wife, I was his taxi on a number of occasions when I passed him walking, still with that air about him, to the Boumarsund Social Club, where it was reported he was still one hell of a dancer at the age of more than three score and 10.

Like all good things, even relationships come to an end. We drifted apart, and the last time I saw him he stood bent and frail at the door to his home. I tooted the horn of my Volkswagen Beetle as I passed, his squinting eyes straining to see whose car had blared out its noisy hello. As he raised his hand weakly, I doubt if he realised it was his young friend, his once constant companion who used to sit with him open-mouthed, listening to every word he said, or accompany him on cold jaunts into the Northumberland countryside, trapping, bird-nesting or taking the occasional pheasant or rabbit.

The mould for countrymen has long since been broken, and they don't make birdmen like Bill Ogle any more and, for these modern, conservation-orientated times, maybe it's for the best. His trapping-type has, however, been replaced by a real ogre – the underground bird-dealer – who only thinks in pounds, shillings and pence, and who has no real love for the birds of which he is custodian. In today's modern, all-knowing society, there certainly wouldn't be a place for Bill's trapping prowess, but for his knowledge and experience with birds, there would always be.

CHAPTER 9

CUD TOWERS

It has been said that God's finger touched, but did not press, in the making of England. Growing up in the English county of Mid Northumberland gave me so much happiness and joy, and the countryside surrounding the Bedlington area held a certain magic and feel all of its own. How I enjoyed those heavenly days, when happy summers beamed warmth and elation that seemed to last forever, and bad-tempered winters decorated the countryside with a cold but handsome blanket of snow that imprisoned us for weeks on end.

My knowledge and awareness of birds and animals was building up encyclopaedically, thanks to continuous gazing through mother nature's shop window and schooling by many of the county's older characters. Like these, I ate, drank and slept wildlife and mused in every bird and animal book I could lay my hands on. While pottering about in the countryside, no week passed without an attempt to secure a mouse hiding under a corrugated sheet of steel, splodge through a stream or pond for amphibian acquaintances or catch one of my feathered friends using a myriad of home-made trapping devices.

One such gadget consisted of a borrowed, metal dust-bin lid, held up with a stick to which a length of string was attached. Small pieces of bread were placed strategically to tempt the wildlings and, when common garden birds such as starlings, house sparrows, song thrushes or robins hopped and searched under its shadow, the cord was pulled and the lid grabbed at the unsuspecting target.

Another unique trapping device came about inadvertently, because a large piece of foliage was missing from the bottom of the tall privet hedge that surrounded a garden across the street from our house. The owner of the garden had temporarily patched up the gap with the aid of some small wire mesh. One winter, when snow fell like envelopes from the heavens and was lying so deep it covered the tops of my Wellingtons, I cleared this gap and, on the exposed soil and sombre dead leaves, I added some ripped up pieces of bread. From the other side of the street, I watched commando-like as hungry birds nervously entered. When there were enough in position, I ran across as fast as I could, slipping and sliding on the snow, then I would dive head-long into the bottom of the bush, hands grabbing at the fleeing birds. Sometimes I would be unsuccessful and seize nothing but a handful of snow or rotten leaves, other times my prize was a lovely, speckled-breasted song thrush, an ebony blackbird or a bad-tempered robin. These little feathered wonders I would study and examine, then excitedly take them to let my mam see my newly-caught wonders. The screams of 'Get that out of here' regularly echoed through the house, down the yard and into the street. I eventually released my captives none the worse for wear. Times like this were among the most blissful in my childhood.

One autumn, I spent my school holidays potato picking for old Joe Binney at Sleekburn Farm. Now, potato picking for a lot of folk was spoken of in reverential rather than affectionate tones, but I loved it. I saved every penny of my 15 shillings-a-day wages and then invested some of it wisely, I

thought, in the purchase of a second-hand bike. This I saw as my passport to travel further afield on solitary trapping expeditions, or to get to my old mates more quickly and easily.

I wasn't tied to my old chums as much as I had been. Like a young buzzard exercising its wings on its first taste of soaring flight, I now concentrated a fair amount of my energies upon venturing out trapping alone. It was on one such jaunt that I happened to meet and make friends with a new birdman and trapper, a real gentleman of the bird world – his name, Cud Towers.

One weekend, I travelled on my recently-acquired bike to Cambois, a mining village situated close to the steel-grey waters of the North Sea. This area was once a thriving metropolis, with cloned rows of dark terraced houses. The close-knit community was employed mainly by the colliery, or the shipyard at Blyth, which was only a short ferry journey away. A great number of these dowdy localities were disappearing as the industries that created them wound down and, on the remaining scarred wasteland, weeds and vermin found a most hospitable and inviting habitat.

On my early morning visit, I was armed with a lively, male goldfinch callbird and a drop-in type trap cage. I was aware that many linnets flocked in this area. I witnessed them regularly in passing, when accompanying my dad in his Albion six-wheel tipper wagon, which proclaimed the words 'As sure as the sun rises' across its bull-nosed front grill. I had also witnessed many beautiful, seven-coloured goldfinches joining together with their drab cousins for communal food-searching and group aerial displays. I was in possession of enough linnets at the time but, as Bill Ogle always said, You can never have enough goldfinch cocks in your shed. I picked an inviting, secluded spot and set to work.

It wasn't too long before I caught my first bird, a male goldfinch. From the rounded tips of its main wing flights and the fact that three feathers on each side of its tail contained pure white patches, I was able to ascertain that this bird was an older adult – a welcome addition nevertheless. Young first-year goldfinches are probably the best to catch, as they usually settle down more easily and adapt quite readily to a new life in captivity. The older birds, however, also have their uses. Most have already bred in the wild with hens of their own kind, but it's amazing how many of these Casanova birds will take a mate that is not of their own kith and kin. They are randy little beggars, who will virtually mate with an outstretched finger if you put your hand in the cage.

Now, apart from the actual catching of birds, my mentors also taught me to be aware of the new threat to our pastime – in the form of those opposed to it. At one time, everyone caught birds, kept a bird's egg collection or possessed a wild singer in the house as a pet. However, legislation had recently been introduced that outlawed all these activities, placing a large part of the population outside the law. These new rulings against activities that had been conducted for centuries could not be expected to work immediately, but there were those who thought they should and who would report any goings-on that were contrary to the Protection of Birds Act at the drop of a deerstalker. Although the police, at this time, viewed such crimes only as nuisance offences, they would still be required to act on any report. So detection was best avoided, if at all possible.

My ever-watchful, hawk-like eyes suddenly detected movement and homed in on the figure of a man in the distance, standing motionless behind a line of bushes. I worked on the premise that, if I knew he was there, he had seen me, so I picked up all my belongings, packed them into the haversack and left my mossy armchair.

I pedalled under cover of the old colliery and along the railway lines with the guile of a fox, all the time looking out for the intruder into my domain, whom I had temporarily lost sight of. As I came up to a cinder track, the man appeared in front of me. His stout figure stood as a barrier, like John Little blocking Robin Hood's path. He didn't move an inch, as my back wheel locked and skidded on the ash when I applied the brakes.

'In a hurry, lad? Did you catch anything?' he asked in an enquiring, but polite, manner.

'Caught? Caught what?'

'Birds! I've watched you every time you've been down here.' I just looked at him, not knowing what to say. I could have made a run for it – he was an old codger and would never have caught me – and violence was never part of any escape plan.

'Don't worry, son. I'm not going to shop you. I do it myself.' He smiled and walked slowly past me. 'I have a birdshed over there,' and he pointed in the general direction of the sea and a short row of yellow-brick, terraced houses where, at the top end, a high baton-fence surrounded a small plot of allotments. As I was to some extent still cornered, I was as leery of this stranger as my old foster dog, Duke, would have been had he been there, but I felt myself giving in to his friendly personality and soft spoken voice.

Any first impressions I held of this old man would certainly never fit the profile expected of a trapper. He was cleanly dressed in a tweed-type jacket and corduroy trousers that were almost wheaten in colour. (Surely, now I had seen every possible shade and colour combination of this type of trousers.) He wore a flat cap too, and glasses, and his overall appearance resembled the landowner, country squire or gentleman farmer.

The never-admit-to-anything teaching receded like an ebb tide, as I blurted out,

'Got one goldie cock.' His reply was not what I expected.

'You should be after linnets. There are hundreds over there,' and he pointed over towards my secret garden.

'I've got plenty of them at home.'

'You can never have too many linnet cocks in your shed,' he replied – now where had I heard something like that before?

'Where do you live, lad?'

'Bedlington Station, beside Kings and Queens Road.'

'Blimey! You're keen! Are there no goldies up there?'

'There are, but I just thought I would have another look down here for a change.'

'Ah! This is one of your secret places, is it?' he said, lifting a finger and tapping it gently on the side of his nose. 'We all have our secret little places.' – Not as secret as I thought, it seemed.

'Anyway, my name is Cud, Cud Towers.'

'I'm Billy Doherty,' I replied politely.

The old man smiled.

'Well now, Billy, I'm going back over home now, and you're quite welcome to come and have a look at my set-up, if you wish.' Only one goldfinch to show for my endeavours but, with such an invitation, the morning wasn't going to be a waste of time after all.

'That would be great,' I said, and we set off slowly along the path carpeted with crunching cinders, while, from both sides of the hawthorn-lined aisle, the bird life that resented our presence twittered angrily as we passed. On our journey, I received a brief synopsis of this man's avian interests: apart from keeping British finches, he was also a keen border canary man; and he continually pointed out items of wildlife interest as we ambled along. Hey, that's my job! I thought to myself.

The interior of his allotment was both tidy and well organised. The high fence was a deterrent for both vagabonds and prying eyes. My first impression was that it was a good place to set a trap cage or two.

Positioned to our right was a large, black shed, with an all-wire-framed outdoor flight attached to the rear exterior wall. At the opposite side of the garden stood a racing pigeon-loft, gloss-painted and clean, resting on raised brick legs. The centre of the plot housed a leek trench and good-sized area for planting vegetables. The soil looked as though it were of good quality and quite sandy – probably due to its location being only a rod-cast away from the beach.

My host opened the main door to his hut and then pushed open the wire safety door. The inside of the shed was as well thought out as his allotment; it was also spotlessly clean, devoid of dust, chaff or spiders' homes. It was without doubt the cleanest birdroom I had ever visited, the creation of a cleanliness fanatic. Every cage was painted light blue and was so fresh looking, which complemented the lucky birds inside. No green algae bred on any water drinker, no dust could be detected with the wipe of a finger on any ledge, and it all gave the impression that if a single piece of wood shaving fell from a cage, Cud would have caught it before it hit the oilcloth-covered floor.

His first task on entering was to open all the windows and

vents, then to sweep up a small number of seed husks that had successfully run the gauntlet to the floor.

'I like my birds to have plenty of fresh air,' he stated proudly. This made the atmosphere in the hut seem very cold indeed, but it didn't affect the inmates at all. In fact, the birds on show were very sleek and tight feathered.

A Mensa award wasn't necessary to work out that he was into exhibiting his birds: a number of wire border canary show cages hung proud of the walls, while others were fastened to stock cage fronts as training cages, in such a way that the birds could go in and out at will. His canaries seemed well rounded and shapely. Now I was a regular visitor to Joe Charlton's shed in Bedlington – Joe was the best border man around in a lot of folk's eyes, and I had learnt many useful pointers from him. In my less than expert opinion, these wee gems in front of me were on a par with what I had seen previously at Bedlington.

Positioned at the bottom end of the shed was a bank of very small cages, too small to be used as breeders. On closer inspection, I found that some of these housed goldfinches, linnets and redpolls.

'They're my packing-down cages,' Cud said in answer to my questioning glance. I stood like a statue, viewing the contents open-eyed.

'Some nice birds there, eh?'

'There sure is,' I replied, never taking my gaze off them for one moment. In one large adjacent cage, I couldn't help noticing a solitary male goldfinch, accompanying what looked like a number of canary hens.

'What's he in there for, Cud?' The old man approached the cage and put his face close to the bars.

'That's my muler. He was caught in three years ago as a

greypate and has produced mules for me every year since.' The female yellow canaries protested at our close inspection with staccato calls; the prince of the harem just stood there, proud and silent.

My own shed at home was fairly well stocked, and a number of breeding seasons were secured under my belt but, although I had tried, mule production for me remained elusive.

'I've never bred a mule, but I have a friend, Jimmy Miller from Bedlington, who has.' Cud's head turned sharply.

'Jimmy the Ragman? I know him. How is the old gypsy? I haven't seen him for years.'

'He's well. Got plenty of linnets in.'

'He's always had a soft spot for a linnet, has old Jimmy,' Cud replied. 'They've always been a favourite of his.'

More examination of the shed revealed a number of greenfinches. 'Did you catch them?'

'No, I bred them in that flight outside. They've all got proper rings on too. I lost a lot of chicks at first. These are the only ones left, but they're looking good.' I couldn't disagree with his statement.

Greenfinches were never my favourite bird. Whenever I set a trap for them in the garden, it would have to be an exceptional individual that I would give room to and feed, but I must admit the large, well-feathered, almost tame examples in front of me caused me to rethink.

The lively lesser redpolls in his possession were also rung with the appropriately sized rings, as were some pleasant looking siskins.

'You must have bred them too?' I asked, pointing to these two diminutive, closely-related species.

'Yes, the siskins went down outside in the same flight as

the greenies; the redpolls bred in a treble canary breeder.'

'Never!' I exclaimed. My disbelief was due to the fact that every bird book, magazine and British bird-breeder advised us novices that finches could only be propagated in spacious well-planted flights. It would seem that, as with all general conclusions and sweeping statements, such assertions were only partly correct. Learning that breeding in this way was possible was to lay the foundations for me as a producer of British finches in smaller environments later in life. In the ensuing decades, I bred almost every common finch in various sized cages, some enclosures down to canary double-breeding dimensions.

My first experience of this birdshed – one I was to worship so much – and of this gentleman's hospitality sadly came to an end as, eventually, I left to return home, but with an open invitation to revisit any time I liked. This was by no means the last time I would sit cracking with this most amiable man.

Old Cud didn't tutor me on the fundamentals of bird-trapping as did some of the other birdmen I was acquainted with did, but he taught me how captive birds and their environments should be kept, and also how to adhere to his philosophy of 'it's nice to be nice'. Surprisingly, Cud and I never travelled out into the fields trapping together as a team. The closest we came to this was when we peered side by side through the net-curtains of his shed towards a trap cage or flap net set among the greenery in his allotment. I did, however, have need of my friend's assistance one cold December morning, when I was once again in the area I arrogantly believed to be my own, pitting my wits and trapping prowess against feeding charms of goldfinches.

My Raffie Gibson-constructed stow box on this end-of-

year outing was beginning to fill up well, and I waited for the next goldfinch to come within earshot of my strategically-placed callbird. In the distance, I spotted a small group of birds lifting and feeding among the wasteland's indigenous wild plant crop. Even at such a distance, I could make out they weren't goldfinches: their flight wasn't the butterfly-like bouncing style of goldfinches, but its manner suggested they were still finches.

As part of the tools of my trade, a pair of binoculars always hung around my neck when I was out in the fields. I raised the eye-glasses to discover the group of birds were redpolls, but not the long-fork-tailed, dark-coloured lessers I was familiar with – these were mealy redpolls, refuelling on our shores after their exhausting flight from Scandinavia. They were much bigger than the peachies endemic to this country and distinctly lighter in colour. As the birds neared my hidy-hole, I began to pick up their call notes. They sounded very similar to their smaller cousins and are probably indistinguishable to the ears of a layman, but my finely-tuned hearing could detect there was a difference.

What a rare opportunity this was! If I could only grab a few of these welcome winter visitors. None of my friends possessed these birds, not even the king of trappers, Bill Ogle; but I was momentarily stumped as to how I could entice them into my trap, when a goldfinch cock was the only caller I had with me. Going back home was out of the question; so was coming back the next day. The redpolls were feeding vigorously, building up their strength after their long journey over the North Sea, before moving further inland; they might not have been there the following day, and I didn't want to miss the opportunity to land some.

Suddenly, a flash of inspiration: Cud! Surely, he would

lend me a redpoll callbird. I quickly packed my gear and sped off on my push-bike, scrambling over embankments and exposed mounds of red shale, which occasionally let out the reek of yellow sulphur. I was quite out of breath as I rattled the knocker of Cud's back door.

'Is Cud in?' I asked the woman that eventually came to the entrance.

'Cud!' she shouted. 'Somebody is here to see you.' The usually immaculately-dressed Cud came out, his open shirt exposing a white string-vest that was doing a damn good job of holding back a large, bloated belly. His braces draped by his side, and he had on a pair of red-chequered, well-worn, but comfortable-looking slippers. My heart pounded on the wall of my chest like a swinging brick. I took a large intake of breath and gasped,

'Cud, there's a load of mealy redpolls over the back. I've only got a goldie with me. Are you going to come with one of your peachies?' The old man stayed calm.

'Take it easy, lad. I'll be with you in a moment.' He turned back into the house and returned shortly, more the man I knew.

'Can't come with you, Billy lad, but you can take one of my redpolls,' he said, as he strode up the short street to his allotment, with me hurriedly pushing my bike to keep up. We entered the shed, and he quickly removed an unco-operative male lesser redpoll from the comfort of its cage.

'Will a lesser drop mealies to the cage?' I asked.

'Should do. If they've just come in, they'll be hungry and their defences will be that much lower because of it.' The frowning bird replaced my goldfinch cock in the tiny centre compartment of the trap cage. I packed it safely into my bag and left.

'Good luck, youngin,' Cud shouted, as I pedalled away. 'I'll leave the shed open, just in case I'm away before you get back.'

With tunnel vision, my journey passed in a blur. I travelled at high speed, with a total disregard for obstacles such as boulders and pot holes. Arriving at my usual place, I quickly undid the straps of my haversack to get the redpoll, who was already calling as I lifted him out of the bag. With nervous fumbling fingers, I set the trap. I could hear the foraging redpolls among the tall, meadow fox-tail grass and the tired, dried-out remains of sow thistle, meadow sweet and dock. I quickly made for my makeshift cover and gazed back excitedly towards the cage. In less than a minute, a small number of redpolls emerged from the dense grass and weeds, alighting on and around my trap. Instantly, one of them dropped in.

Should have had a flap net here, I immediately thought to myself, and I ran over, removed the captive, resetting the device with the little finch held securely in one hand. For a moment, I sat there examining the first mealy redpoll I had ever held, but this was not a time for study, and I slinked back and put the bird in the stow box. These alien visitors gave me a clambering display of their vivaciousness and also showed me how very tame they were. Some had moved only a few yards away from the trap, when disturbed by the removal of its first victim, but it wasn't long before they regathered and returned. Then, once again, and with no hesitation, another was in the bag. This was all too easy and, within an hour, I had secured practically the whole group of 14. A lack of storage space, however, put an end to my morning's work.

I returned to Cud's house, but the old man was nowhere

to be found. The shed, as he had said, was unlocked. I shep-
herded the redpolls into a pre-prepared canary double-breeding cage, and added a shallow water receptacle, as Jimmy the
Ragman had once advised me to do with any newly-trapped
birds. There were no food or water containers in any of the
other cages in this spotless birdroom – this was Cud's method to help avoid contamination and disease – but I didn't
want to lose any birds through their not finding water, not
because of any potential monetary value, but because, as a
bird-lover, I hated to witness disease or suffering in any of
the wards in my possession, caught in or otherwise.

From the confines of another cage, the red faces of the
goldfinches I had caught earlier stared up at me with pen-
etrating, dark eyes. Although looking a little nervous, they
were no worse for wear and, after better scrutiny, I established there were some nice birds among them. For his help,
I decided to leave all the birds caught that morning in the
cages where they were settling, so that Cud could pick out
anything he fancied, before I moved the rest back to my
place. My inquiring mind also wanted some information
about these new redpolls, and the old man would probably
be able to satisfy my instinctive what-where-and-why crav-
ing.

Later that afternoon, I once again biked back down towards the windy coast, my legs never leaving off their pump-
ing action for a break or rest. Cud was pottering about in his
garden, as I arrived. He turned when he heard the loud click
of the gate's latch, paused and eyed me for a moment.

'There's some bloody nice redpolls in there,' he said, obviously impressed and enthusiastic about the quality of my
morning's catch. We entered the hut and I noticed immediately that all the birds were sorted out. The obvious crim-

son-breasted, perky male redpolls displayed themselves in the sanctuary of their temporary accommodation and were more interested in their food receptacles than in the two sets of ogling eyes passionately giving them the once-over.

'I've sorted them out for you,' said Cud, as he stooped to wipe a small amount of scattered seed from the shed floor. I proudly examined these living possessions that filled me with such euphoria.

'You'll be proud of that little haul?' he said, taking a quick glance into the cages.

'Yes, I am. You can have half them, if you want, Cud,' I offered willingly, as I went to sit on the soft bench seat. 'I wouldn't have got any, if it wasn't for your help.'

'Don't be silly, lad. But I will take a pair; and there's a nice goldie cock I wouldn't mind, to replace my muler.' I was puzzled and promptly glanced towards the goldfinch male that had served him so well over the last few seasons as a producer of hybrids. He was still in with his harem, hounding the canary hens with his usual bossiness.

'He's still there,' I said. The old man looked at me, his eyes unable to hide their smile through the lenses of his glasses.

'How many mules have you bred?' he asked, with feigned reservation in his voice.

'None.'

'Well, the goldie cock is now yours. Take him! If you don't breed any with him, you never will as long as you have a hole in your arse.' I couldn't believe my ears.

'I can't, Cud, he's your muler! Are you sure?' My narrow protests were useless, and he turned to ignore me. I was torn between the idea of possessing a virtually guaranteed hybridising goldfinch – a bird that I had always admired, my first port of call whenever I entered Cud's second home – and the feeling that I was stealing something special from this old man, a treasure I would never have parted with had he been mine.

'Any goldie will mule, lad. Now get him out, before I change my mind.' Such an act of sheer kindness affected me greatly and brought tears to my eyes.

All my birds, including the goldfinch, were placed into a number of boxes and packed carefully into my haversack. Cud granted me a solitary wave and half a smile, then, with firmly-planted strides, turned and went to finish his gardening duties. I left quickly to beat the tide of evening darkness that was slowly but surely drawing in. I pedalled furiously past the four giant, grey towers of the Blyth Power Station, which stared down their noses at me. In the main, my journey was a haze, the result of the excitement of thinking about what was in my bag.

Finally, I reached my objective, home, and in my shed I filled the cages with the birds they so eagerly awaited. The goldfinch cock, the new jewel in the crown of my hut, was presented with a palace of his own. Once everything was sorted, with food and water in every cage, I sat alone staring at my birds, recording in my mind every movement, every detail until darkness forced me to leave.

Acts of generosity like Cud's were not isolated incidents among the birdmen that were part of my youth. Instilled into all of them were the traits of giving and helping. Cud's own generous gesture in offering me the muling goldfinch cock kick-started my successful hybrid-breeding plans. In the following season, I produced no less than three clutches of mules.

I was a good and faithful friend of Cud Towers right up to

my late teens. I was lucky to start my first job – a vocational apprenticeship – within spitting distance of his well-serviced gardens, so I visited him almost every lunch-break. After a period of two years, with my mind set on higher things, I left the job. Although the move produced many opportunities for me in the transport industry, how sadly I missed my daily, hour-long sit in Cud's shed!

The wind of change was also beginning to bite harder into the ways of those who trapped birds. The threat of heavy fines drained the excitement and romance from the pastime, and those who had taught me the old ways so unselfishly were disappearing one by one. I no longer ventured into Cud's domain, where pollutant-spewing factories replaced the feeding grounds of birds and rabbit burrows and busy roads replaced the marshy homes of newt, frog and toad.

Who really commits wildlife crimes? It seems that the old man that catches a few wildlings will always be blamed and thus persecuted, while the cruel tyrant called progress marches on, destroying mother nature's treasures in its wake.

The local bird shows became the last bastion where my old friend Cud and I would meet; but we drifted apart naturally, until I no longer saw him. Years later, I heard from a friend that Cud had passed away, a fact that really saddened me.

There were birdmen and there were birdmen in my life, and then there was Cud Towers. And then he left for the big flight in the sky. What a gentleman he was! A man who showed such generosity and who always taught me that 'it's nice to be nice'.

CHAPTER 10

WALTER ETHERAGE

I remember well how unconventional my first-ever meeting with Walter was. While walking home from playing a game of football, with my size-five, leather 'caser' tucked securely under my arm, I passed what turned out to be his house. Stopping suddenly, I watched attentively as this man lifted bundles of dead woodpigeons from the back of a car, the limp, blue–grey carcases tied together at their necks with orange twine. A long gun rested across his shoulder, while down his back hung a bulging, canvas shooting-bag.

For a second his head lifted from his task, and his gaze drifted in my direction, instantly noticing my curiosity.

'Give us a hand, youngin. Don't just stand there,' he rapped in a drill-sergeant manner. I was pretty well taken aback by the sudden command, but eagerly threw my ball into the long grass of the front garden and began to lift some pigeons, two heavy bundles in each hand from the car's wide-open boot. There was none of the conventional formalities, none of the 'Hi, there! Pleased to make your acquaintance. My name's Billy Doherty.'

I carried the carcases through a door that led into a narrow passageway, the whitewashed walls dusting my clothes, as I squeezed past the bulky figure stiffly removing the bag from his back.

'Just put them down there,' the man said, pointing to a

pile already lying on the cold, concrete floor, which acted as a natural cooler for the freshly-killed meat. Incredulously, I inspected the feathery mound. Never had I seen so many dead pigeons in one place, or realised how beautiful a bird a powdery, rose-breasted ring-dove is.

'Did you shoot them?' I asked, hoping for an informative story on how he had obtained so many.

'Yes, a friend and I have been up country.' He placed the shotgun through the open door of a friendly-smelling scullery. 'Do you want to take some of these cushats† home for your dad?' I had never heard my father mention eating pigeons, but to a man whose wartime fare had been enhanced by such culinary items as badger steaks, moorhen, pewit eggs and goat's milk, these would probably be seen as delicacies.

'Cushats?' I said, in a questioning tone of voice. He bent forward, picked two bundles from the heap and, like a game-dealer, expertly felt some of the plump breasts, squeezing them with his strong-looking hands. At the same time, he explained that this local nickname was derived from coo or cow-shits, as these birds were notorious for consuming cow-dung when the winters were hostile and food hard to find.

'There now. Some good uns among them,' he said, as he passed the bundle over. For a moment, I stood proudly with the string handles gripped tightly: these were for my dad, and nothing would be able to prise them from the vice-like grip of my fingers.

From behind another door that led into the rear garden, my ears detected the unmistakeable, musical twittering of goldfinches.

† the ring-dove or woodpidgeon

'What's up, lad? Too heavy?'

'No, they're ok. It's just I can hear goldfinches in your back garden.'

'Blimey! What the hell have you got for lugs?'

'I keep birds,' I told him.

'Birdman, eh? Well, you better come with me.' – The tone of his voice like that of a teacher pleased at the satisfactory progress of one of his pupils, and he led me unhurriedly into the sanctuary of his private grounds.

The garden was fairly large, totally grassed, with a single spreading tree that played peek-a-boo from behind a tidy, green-painted shed. The main door of the hut was wide open and, behind it, was a meshed safety door.

'Wow! You keep birds too!' I exclaimed. He replied with a twisted wink, a cock of his head and a raw smile, as though he had tricked me in some way.

A snapped clothes-peg pushed through a hasp on the door was removed, and I followed humbly into the confines of this brightly-painted out-shed. It wasn't a large hut, but the interior was well laid out to accommodate as many cages as possible. These cages were small in comparison to those of other birdmen I was acquainted with. The area of what was the back wall was completely covered in diminutive cages, too small as breeding environments, more for housing a single bird for 'steadying down' or show training purposes. Hanging on the far wall were three banks of canary-sized breeding cages. There were no flights at all in the shed.

I closed the wire door behind me and searched for some form of latch to secure it. A thick arm brushed me aside as the bloke stretched and fastened a small, wire hook through a strategically-placed staple in the frame of the door.

'There now, have a seat. What's your name anyway?'

'Billy,' I replied. 'Billy Doherty.'

'Mine's Walter. You're not John Doherty's son, are you?' My eyes were temporarily snatched from the cages.

'Yes, do you know him?'

'Well, of course I know him. I worked at the Station Pit with him. I know nobody better. He was one of the best putters in the mine,' he said, with a smile in his voice. I wasn't too surprised, as I had yet to meet someone who didn't know my dad. Once again, my eyes returned to the cages, and I stared intensely into their depths, every one of them holding a secret.

'They're all goldfinches,' I said, disbelievingly.

'Yes, lad. Love my goldies. There are some goldie mules further along.' I inched the length of the shed, examining the contents of every cage. He was obviously a trapper, but what was he going to do with all these, I thought to myself. There were around 20 male goldfinches, about half a dozen golden-masked mule-birds and not a canary in sight.

'You've got no canaries.'

'No, I don't like them. They are disease carriers. I get a couple of hens in for the breeding season to raise some mules, then throw them out when I'm finished with them – spoil the mules' song, they do.'

'I thought you might have bought the mules off Jimmy Miller. He breeds mules too,' I said, just to impress him that I had friends in the know. Walter coughed and spluttered, like a dog choking on a piece of broad grass.

'That old bugger!' he yelled, laughingly. 'He hasn't bred a mule in his life! He gets them all from me. Is that what he's told you: he breeds them?' Oops! Looked like I had dropped my old mate in it a bit!

Walter was still shaking his head in disbelief, when a voice from outside called,

'Walter, do you want a cup of tea?'

'Yes, love,' he shouted, 'and a drink of pop for the laddo here.' Just then, a woman peered into the shed.

Every young lad has adolescent fantasies about an older woman at some time during his life, and I was no exception to this healthy rule. This can be a next door neighbour, a friend's mother or a woman serving in the local shop. I may have already mentioned my penchant for my school teacher, Miss Waddington, but I did have another for the postie that delivered letters to my parents' house. Such ardour wasn't confined to me and, if I were playing football on the local field with my mates and she passed, we would stop with the traffic lights on red, our senses standing to attention, observing her every gliding step till out of sight. Then, with a sigh, we would continue our game, no worse for wear. I mention this because the goddess staring me full in the face was none other than the postie wife.

'Well, do you want some pop?' her gentle voice asked. Stuttering, I answered,

'Uh, uh, yes, please, uh, love to, I mean love some.' She smiled a heavenly smile and left, my eyes following close behind, locked on the sight of her perfectly-rounded bottom sticking through her flowery pinny.

'That's the wife,' Walter said, as bird-talk was resumed, while I stole glimpses of her at every opportunity. 'What were we on about again?' he asked, scratching his head. 'Oh! I remember – the Ragman.' And once again he began to laugh. 'Mule breeder indeed! Wait till I see him!'

It was obvious from the lack of flights that Walter wasn't the breeder of the goldfinches in his possession, but there were no obvious tell-tale signs of him being an illicit trapper. All my rogue and vagabond friends had trap cages, nets or tubes of lime-covered wand sticks displayed in an act of defiance on their shed walls, all advertising that they were trappers. None of those ensnaring tools were evident here. So to appease my curiosity, pointing at the birds in the cages, I asked cautiously,

'Do you catch these?' He turned, looked at me and smiled.

'I could say no, but then I would be telling lies. If you know who you say you know, you'll have already worked out that I like to dabble in a spot of catching.' Looking keenly over the number of birds, I thought to myself: A spot of catching! That was an understatement, if ever there was one.

Goldfinches were also my favourites, but I revelled in catching other common finches, pitting my still-wet-be-hind-the-ears trapping skills against redpolls, linnets, bullfinches and siskins.

'Don't you go out for anything else,' I asked.

'I did at one time, but goldfinches are the only birds I trap now. I live on a regular flight path for them, and most of the time get what I want here: the garden's my field and the house is my hedge-back. There are a few folk locally that try to take advantage of this natural abundance of goldies and beat me to them, but I have a secret weapon,' and he pointed to the lime tree behind the hut. 'When the birds travel up from the river, they run a gauntlet of callers. They are lured down and, for a split second, can't make their minds up whose garden to visit. Then, they see my tree, and that's it! They land and they are halfway to being mine – the boys further down the estate hate me for it.'

It was still in my mind that I hadn't seen any trapping devices.

'What do you use for catching,' I asked.

'Well, in the garden I use a drop-in trap cage or clap net. Out in the fields, I either use these, or the wands, depending where I am.'

My attention was distracted again as his wife brought out refreshments: a large pot of tea for Walter, a plastic beaker of lemonade for yours truly, and a plate of biscuits: Blue Ribands, Mint Yoyos and those chocolate-covered, triangular-shaped wafer ones. What a smile she possessed! I'm sure she secretly fancied me – maybe not; this was an era long before the advent of toyboys and the like, I think. I believe it was Mark Twain who said, 'You can't depend on your eyes when your imagination is out of focus.'

After a while, the aroma of Sunday dinner cooking that drifted silently on an invisible serving-plate from Walter's house reminded me that it was getting on and time to go. My bundles of woodpigeons were packed into a large brown paper sack, whose original function in life had been to transport potatoes. I carried my empty cup and scored brownie points as I passed it to the postie wife's delicate hand.

'By! He's a canny lad,' she said. I could feel the colour rushing to my face, which in turn triggered a proud smile. I picked up my ball from the front garden as I left and made off, heavily laden, to the call of 'come back again', an invitation I regularly took up, as I had more than one reason to visit Walter Etherage's home again.

CHAPTER 11

GOLDIES GALORE

I was taught to be a good, nay, successful hunter, and that knowing everything possible about the traits and habits of the intended quarry is of paramount importance, a tenet that, for me, has stood the test of time.

It was during my trapping learning-curve that I adopted the same principle, diligently building up personal profiles of the common finches I wished to catch. I read books on my subjects avidly and visited various countryside locations, where I would sit for hours and observe their antics.

On a number of occasions, my early morning wanderings took me to a very large thistle patch, in fields bathing in the shadows of the black, iron railway bridge that spanned the River Blyth, between Bedlington and the village of Bebside. On each visit, I eagerly studied a charm of goldfinches seeking their breakfast among prickly white and purple plumes. I watched as these birds nipped between bulging thistle heads, extracting the large seeds which are high in proteins, oil and amino-acids. Regular observation also revealed that the group's number was increasing. The findings from my reconnaissance missions were reported to Walter, and a plan was prepared to obtain some of the beautiful birds from this flock.

It was mid October when Walter and I tramped the stubble at the crack of dawn towards the goldfinches' banqueting table. Flocks of tree sparrows, chaffinches and greenfinches were already taking full advantage of the field's hidden pantry; they lifted well in front of us, alerted by the swishing sound of our strides.

We peered through hawthorn hedges, recently washed and bejewelled with ruby berries.

'Christ, lad! That's some thistle patch!' For a moment, I was filled with glum apprehension.

'Is it too big?' Walter scratched his head roughly, searching for an answer.

'No, we'll not let it beat us. Come on, I have a plan.' We pressed backwards through the hedge to escape its prickly lashes and stumbled into the field.

'Put the gear down on the grass,' Walter ordered. Our paraphernalia consisted of a goldfinch callbird in a small wire cage, some carrying boxes and hessian bags. Walter began to demolish the tall thistles violently with his stick.

'Come on, Billy. Break them all down, and just leave a small number standing in the centre.'

I needed no second bidding. This was great fun, and I danced a merry jig, stamping the plants down to the ground with my feet. We continued until there was an approximately six-foot-round area remaining. Although I was, for the moment, as happy as a fiddler's bitch after our little weed-clearing exercise, I still hadn't worked out why we were doing it.

Walter trod back slowly towards our trapping equipment, collecting the cage and callbird and returning to the fresh ruins of the once thistle fortress. The cage was placed on the ground of what was the north side, facing back towards the hawthorn hedge. Tacky wand sticks were removed from a container pulled from Walter's inside pocket and fixed at well-spaced intervals on the tops of the plants left standing.

Ah! Now I was beginning to see what he was up to. Birds coming in for food would always go to plants that were still standing three feet off the ground, as opposed to those broken and lying flat. That is a trait of these birds, preferring to sway on high plant-tops of thistle or teasel, stripping the seed pods, while keeping an ever-watchful eye on activities around them. They would, however, take to being ground feeders on occasion, when chickweed was in flower or when the heart-shaped seeds of shepherd's purse were ripe and inviting; but, given a choice, they would always choose the tall seat at the bar.

With the ambush in place, we lay in wait amid the dense hawthorn hedge.

'That was a good idea, Walter, knocking them thistles down. Do you think it will work?'

'Should do. I remember using a similar ploy a while back to good effect.' Walter lay one of the hessian sacks on the ground and adjusted his seating arrangement with a wriggle of his backside. 'We just have to wait and see if your flock of goldies turn up now.' Could that have been an element of doubt I detected in his voice, I wondered.

Something I had learnt during my somewhat short association with wild bird-trapping was that, if you observed a group of goldfinches feeding in a particular area at a certain time of day, odds on they would frequent the same area at the same time over the next few days, or at least until their supplies were exhausted. So I was quietly confident that my monitored group would keep their appointment.

We sat quietly gossiping, idly chit-chatting about scandals and rumours in the local bird world, at the same time maintaining a constant vigil with eyes and ears across the fields toward the mist-veiled treetops of the Halfpenny Woods. Meanwhile, we were audience to a concert, with players on all sides, including a song-thrush, wren, hedge-accentor and robin, all giving individual musical renditions that harmonised perfectly into the finished production. A nervous rabbit emerged from the sanctuary of a well-hidden burrow and made its way in a nose-twitching, unhurried shamble towards the broken-down thistle bed. Walter did a Davy Crocket impression, raising an invisible rifle to his eye. The rabbit's inborn wariness of possible trouble brewing soon made it bolt at high speed back to the long grass, as though scared by his own shadow. Walter's pretend aim was true as he followed the fleeing creature.

'Blam, blam,' he uttered, 'Got him.' For now, however, death was not to be a part of this serene location, and our attention switched back to the reason for our being there.

Together, we glanced up at the grey sky as a solitary goldfinch flew overhead, his calls immediately answered by the Judas bird on the ground. Down the singing dot in the sky dropped, dipping and bouncing on his bumpy decent towards the thistles. The goldfinch glanced like a ricocheting arrow off the top of a thistle head, struck by the finger of an outstretched wand. Wands are usually fixed loosely so that they are pulled out completely by the bird, which will then fall to the ground, the stick ensnared across its wing and body. This tacky stick, however, tipped over and was snagged, unable to be dislodged by the weight of the bird. On spotting this, I bolted from the confines of our well-hidden camp, running as fast as the rabbit we had seen earlier. The goldfinch was hanging by one wing and was sliding slowly out of the wand's gluey grasp. If the bird had struggled just a little, he would have been free. In an instant, I grabbed him from the stick, like a bear swiping a salmon from fast-flowing waters. I had him, and what a bird it was! A first-rate specimen of a male goldfinch. Walter brushed past me and set another wand, and we both quickly returned to our hiding-place.

I hadn't done a lot of catching with wands yet, but I had heard that bird-lime on feathers could be a real bastard to clean off. This bird, due to the unusual way he was caught, was practically clean; the small amount of glue present on the tip of one wing was scraped off between Walter's front teeth and spat onto the grassy floor.

'There now, as good as old,' said Walter.

'How would you have cleaned him up, if he had been covered,' I asked.

'Well, some people use petrol or various solvent cleaners, but I scrape off as much as I can; and if there's any feathers heavily contaminated, I just carefully pull them out. The newly caught may resemble a burst couch for a short while, but the feathers will grow back – then they'll be no worse for the experience.' Walter took one last expert look before stuffing the bird unceremoniously into a carrying box. 'That's a lovely goldie cock, Billy lad. We could do with some more like him. That was a quick bit of thinking back there. Well done.' These were words I really appreciated, especially coming from a person I considered to be well up in the bird-trapping hierarchy.

A short period of time that felt like a long period of time elapsed before another straggler goldfinch hit our wands. We weren't to have the same luxury of this bird not getting too fouled up with bird-lime, and Walter was able to demonstrate the fundamentals of cleaning a really soiled bird to me. Feathers were stripped out between forefinger and thumb, and the dark grey downiness was rolled into a solid ball and flicked into the bushes.

'There now, that'll do for now. When we get home, we can fix it up better.' That bird was also deposited into the box, which was placed into a dark sack to stop any noisy fluttering.

Walter's eyes widened, alerting me there was something amiss. An index finger to his lips commanded absolute silence, and his pointing directed me to the reason. Beyond the thistles, approaching like a winged army of nymphs and dryads, was the flock we had been waiting for.

'Goldies,' I whispered excitedly. Walter answered with two rapid nods of his head. We slunk down and waited for their imminent arrival, which was due, not to our callbird's luring chant, but more to the fact that the group had frequented this feeding area many times before, as my detective work had already established.

The flock was now feeding on rose-bay willow herb, nipple-wart and dock along the edge of the hedgerow leading to our hide. That is one of the many splendours of mother nature's larder: there is so much choice, allowing the wildlings a varied diet to help maintain optimum health.

Closer and closer they got, playing a carduelan version† of leap-frog as they advanced. Then, the moment we, as trappers, had been waiting for: their foraging switched from the hedgerow to the remains of the thistle patch. It was a fairly large breakaway group from the main flock initially that headed towards the thistles. They were there in an instant.

The first wave hit the wands and several birds fell as

† finch version

though they had been shot, their golden flights spread help-lessly across the sticky wands. This was nothing like the traps or flap nets that I was used to in order to take groups of birds – there was no luxury of delaying, knowing the catch was safe. These birds were stuck, and swift action was required to ensure that the minimum amount of harm and stress befell them. Stress and shock can be major factors determining the survival of newly caught-in birds.

Simultaneously, Walter and I lifted from our seats. Some of the caught birds were bouncing over the grass with wands attached, others lay motionless, staring up at us with plead-ing eyes as we approached.

'Grab the runners,' Walter called out, thinking my youth-ful agility was more suited to this task. I remember finding this a most awkward challenge: handling a single bird and wand with two hands is bad enough, but several birds in each hand borders on the limits of what is physically pos-sible. The wands were spaced out, one between two fingers, to keep the birds apart.

Turning to Walter, I saw him kneeling, in front of him a number of goldfinches lying with attached sticks pointing skywards, like toffee-apples on a tray. Walter beckoned with his hand.

'Bring yours here,' he said in a quiet, but firm, tone. I watched as he took them from me one by one, removed the sticks and placed each bird into a carrying box, which he had remembered to bring along in our rush from the hedge, but which I had forgotten in the excitement. Walter's tech-nique was so methodical and skilled. Within seconds, all eight birds were secure – this was my cue to run and fetch the other boxes from the bushes.

We knelt shoulder to shoulder, sorting out the remaining birds, and put any removed wands in a small pile. For the moment, these sticks resembled feather-decorated Red Indian war-lances, albeit in miniature form. When all the birds were accounted for, the wand sticks were cleaned of all their feathers and pieces of grass. I was in the process of counting them, when my mentor began,

'Always count the number you have put down—'

'And count the number you pick up. I know, I know!'

'Ah! The Ragman is maybe a better teacher than I haven't been giving him credit for,' he laughed.

'Are we going to set them again, Walter? It's still quite early.'

'Goldies are fickle, lad. The ones up there in the trees will have got a scare, seeing their friends falling. We might get the odd straggler, but it's really not worth it.' He had already made his decision that it was time to leave and was beginning to sort our gear. 'We can give it another go tomorrow, if you want.' This more than compensated for the disappointment at having to leave these idyllic surroundings.

We did return the following morning and made a few more lucrative visits after that. Walter and I took more than enough goldfinches using the wands. This was his, but not always my, preferred catching method. I was a trapper, a netter, a trap-cage man and not very keen on wands and bird-lime. Apart from my excursions with the postie wife's husband, I rarely ever used the glue-covered sticks again. I have always seen myself as a bird-lover first and foremost, and the wands have a cruel aspect to them.

CHAPTER 12

REVELATIONS

It has always been my belief that our mid-1900s, bird-friendly ancestors should be given more credit than they have been. We now live at a time when we are governed by laws both of statute and of science. Although they strived after the health and success of the birds in their custody no less than we do, our forebears kept birds in a more natural way and were successful with it. Perhaps theirs was a safer and surer method.

In our birdsheds, we now have generations of aviary-bred specimens to breed from and manage, to establish strains from, form carefully thought-out breeding plans and crossbreed to produce some wonderful hybrid birds – much of which was elusive to breeders in the past. The old birdmen used only raw materials: birds caught from the wild were expected to produce the goods. In some cases, success was achieved, but not to the extent expected today.

The men I have highlighted here are only a sample of those that were involved in taking birds from the wild and keeping them in captivity over two score years ago. They emanated from one geographical location – nowhere special – just a typical Northern England mining area, but their kind has been found throughout the world.

As I walked with these giants, I couldn't help but gain knowledge of their ways, factual drops in a pool of learning in a hobby I believe I have acquired some expertise in. Their traditions are a continual source of inspiration, and I have employed many of their instructions during the time I have been involved in aviculture.

Science, however, is a measurable component for attaining success in bird-keeping, and only a fool would say otherwise. For many years, I have taken what I have learnt about wildlings and their individual characteristics and blended it with the scientific knowledge at our disposal, linking the old ways to the new in a unique nostrum, which has tended to bring success in areas where a lot of modern-thinking contemporaries fall short.

I am leery by nature, always cagey of new ideas that others have so much enthusiasm for. However, I often wonder what old Raffie would think of the beautiful hybrids that I and many others have produced, or how Bill Ogle would view the excellent examples of aviary-bred British birds now on show at the exhibitions he once provided for. These are just two examples of how blending the old and the new has paid dividends.

The catching of wild birds in Great Britain is now banned, and my book in no way reflects what is happening in our countryside today. It is more a graphic account of what transpired during the 1950s and 1960s, an historical and personal view that hopefully illustrates what went on during this period. It is equally important to note that any current, illegal trapping activities have no relation whatsoever to what I have experienced and now documented – that would be like comparing stealing a bottle of milk from a doorstep to robbing a bank.

I did trap birds as a lad, and I enjoyed the thrill of hearing the click of a trap cage or the grabbing swish of a clap net; and, if it were not for current legislation, maybe I would still be practising today. However, being a disciple of experienced birdmen didn't simply educate me in their trapping ways, and, within these pages, I have endeavoured to show that I also bear the mark of a lover of the countryside and of all God's creatures. I know what it is to explore quiet country lanes, walk Scottish moors and Northumberland fells and become intimate with the creatures that see such places as their own.

Fate decreed that I should be taught the ways of the countryside and wild lands, and possess the hunter's guile and ability to ensnare bird and beast. Many decades ago mother nature's riches stole my heart, but it was my very soul they wished to possess.

Throughout my life, birds and the countryside have been an inspiration for me. Many of my experiences are now distant memories. Outside, dark clouds have gathered and a cold wind may blow, but such experiences are part of our inheritance, there for others to view and perhaps be educated and entertained by. Older fanciers may well appreciate my sentiments. Younger ones, or those who have just branched into the hobby, may not.

I conclude by expressing my hope that this book will afford some form of reward to those who have chosen to read it, perhaps because the subject is one of interest to them or one they wish to look into. I have found it a joy to write, although it would have been impossible without the characters that made my childhood such a memorable one and without my late father, who supported and encouraged me from the day I was born to the day he died.

I hope that a time may come when I can write again of my early life and of its many exciting episodes, a few of which go to make up the chapters of this book. For the time being, I look to the birds in my shed and the wildlings in the clear, indigo sky for solace, as these for me lighten the routine of everyday life, sometimes releasing those distant memories of times when I really did have a bird in the hand.

BIRDS

Bullfinches gorging on ebony brambles
Chaffinches squabbling on slender bough
Linnets swaying on spiny gorse bush
Goldfinches dancing around thistles of sow

Kestrel hangs, watching for movement
Owl glides silent in the dead of the night
Sparrowhawk skimming hedges of hawthorn
Buzzard high-soaring on motionless flight

Pheasants resplendent in full royal attire
Partridges bickering over lands and domain
Ptarmigan clad for the winter in ermine
Red grouse guarding the moors in the rain

Lapwings dog-fighting above green pastures
Dunlins racing against wave's ebb and flow
Curlews high-circling fells, hills and valleys
Redshanks' alarm call warning intruders to go

Birds of the garden, birds of the park
Birds of the daytime, birds of the dark
All for a reason, all here to stay
All need protection or they will dwindle away

Bill Doherty

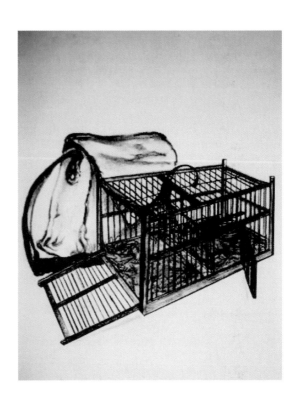